An Old Lady's Writing Tips

An Old Lady's Writing Tips

Reva Spiro Luxenberg

To order additional copies of this book, contact:
Xlibris
1-888-795-4274
www.Xlibris.com
Orders@Xlibris.com
771270

CONTENTS

DEDICATION

To aspiring writers,
and to my husband,
Dr. Edward R. Levenson,
for his love, support, and
skilled editing of this book.

CHAPTER 1

Attitude

I STARTED WRITING when I was in the first grade, and it was an uphill climb. There I was awkwardly grasping a yellow pencil trying my darndest to make two slanted lines meet at the apex with a horizontal bridge in the middle. My *A* was bent out of shape, but it was mine. I had begun my career as a writer.

Stephen King, in his book *On Writing*, describes how his mother encouraged him at an early age. Due to illness King spent most of his first-grade year at home when he should've been in school. He began to write his own stories copying comics almost word for word. When he showed his stories to his mother, she was incredulous that her son was so smart. When she learned that he had copied most of the stories, she said, "Write one of your own, Stevie," and he did.

If you want to write, you don't need a mother to pat you on the back. Though my mother was doting, she never encouraged me to write or, later to go to college. If you have the right attitude, you can write on your own.

Let me tell you about my idea of success. It's not making money with your writing. It's enjoying the writing itself.

Not only did Stephen King say, "Writing isn't about making money." He put it much more compellingly than that, "In the end, it's about enriching the lives of those who will read your work, and enriching your own life as well."

Ernest Hemingway was quoted in *Ernest Hemingway on Writing*, "I have to write to be happy whether I get paid for it or not."

I was a school social worker and I started to write in earnest the last year before my retirement. With the oodles of money from all my books I have earned only enough to pay one month's telephone bill. My pittances never stopped me from writing. Arthritis in my knees and back may have stopped me from playing golf, but not from writing. If you're driven to write, nothing will stop you. One exception is health. When Stephen King was badly injured in an automobile accident in 1999, it slowed him down for a while, but with his determination he returned to the craft.

Many folks have approached me saying that they led unusual lives and wanted to write about their experiences, but didn't know how. That's sad. I think if each had said, "I'd like to play the piano, but I don't know how," I would have answered readily, "Find yourself a piano teacher and take lessons." Writing *can* be learned. You don't have to write a novel that ends up on *The New York Times* bestseller list. It can be your unique memoir—even with grammar and spelling mistakes.

Ernest Hemingway was one of the worst spellers I have ever come across. His spelling, of course, was corrected by an editor before his books got published. In his will he directed that none of his private letters were to be published.

   REVA SPIRO LUXENBERG

I sometimes wonder if it was because he was self-conscious about his spelling. The letters were published in *Ernest Hemingway on Writing* exactly as they were written without any corrections. I was troubled by this violation of his will, as I wouldn't want my journals to be published; but, on the other hand, his letters reveal much about his life that we wouldn't know if his letters hadn't been divulged.

I was shocked seeing the spelling mistakes—but I shouldn't have been. My own son, who was brilliant and had an IQ of 160, was a poor speller. He could run rings around me intellectually. He died when he was thirty-eight. My loss, incidentally, didn't stop me from writing, but it did take me thirteen years afterwards to finish *The Cereal Killer*.

If you want to get your juices flowing like seltzer at an ice cream fountain, it's a good idea to read many different kinds of books—from popular novels to classics. Stephen King had a "Prime Rule." He wrote, "Write a lot and read a lot." He lists about 138 books that he's read and liked. Ernest Hemingway, in a reflection of what books are necessary for a writer to have read, mentioned to a friend approximately thirty-two outstanding books. It's interesting to note that the only book in common on Hemingway's and King's lists is Leo Tolstoy's *War and Peace.* I hadn't read it and ordered it on Amazon. I started it, but it's not my cup of French vanilla tea. I put it next to my other books to read in the future, or maybe in the next world.

In elementary school I wasn't interested in history or geography. I couldn't grasp arithmetic. Recently my husband attempted unsuccessfully to teach me how to do percentages. But I always liked to read. For my first reading task I made out the words on the Corn Flakes cereal box on the kitchen table. Next I graduated to comic books like *Superman* and also to *The Bible* in comic book form. One year I received a collection of books about children in foreign lands. I was fascinated by the Eskimo children, although I never liked cold weather. When I was in the third grade, the teacher announced, "Students, please bring in a present for a grab bag." I don't remember what I brought, but I received Charles Dickens' *A Christmas Carol.* It was too difficult for me to read. Later when I was in the sixth grade, I was able to read it with ease and I enjoyed it.

Ruth Gruber, a humanitarian American photo-journalist, was the youngest person who earned a Ph.D. She was only twenty. She wrote nineteen outstanding books. She died at 105, beating my mother by one year. When she was interviewed in her nineties, she said, "If you want to write—read, read, read."

You don't have to aim for the stars. If you want to write—and obviously you do since you're reading this book—you can start with baby steps. Keep a journal. Journaling is writing. I heard a psychologist say that to sleep more peacefully you should enter in your journal what's disturbing you. He added that your bedroom needs to be cool and dark.

A few years ago in my senior center I was part of a group who wrote a newsletter. The gracious woman who volunteered to lead us left after a few years. She gave everyone in the group a gift. I consider the one I got particularly unique. It's *642 Things to Write About.* Thirty-five writers from the San Francisco Writers' Grotto contributed to this journal. It has prompts at the top of blank rectangles of different sizes of a full page, a half-page, or a quarter-page. It's still available and

I recommend it highly for your getting your creative juices flowing. Every morning after my shower I fill in a prompt. I don't dare to tell my doctor that I don't exercise my limbs, but with these prompts I do get enjoyable exercise for my mind.

Many scholars regard Leonardo da Vinci, the Italian Renaissance polymath, as one of the most diversely talented—or "well-rounded"—individual who ever lived. He was known primarily as a painter, but his notes display an enormous range of interests. Most of his writings are in mirror-image cursive. This could be because he was left-handed. So if you say you can't write well because you write with your left hand, don't use that excuse. Leonardo wrote detailed lists of groceries and lists of money borrowed from him. I don't expect you all to be so meticulous, but I do think the list-keeping strengthened his power of organization and helped him unclutter his mind.

I can't count how many people have informed me seriously that they have no imagination.

Poppycock.

Every human being has an imagination, though not like Leonardo's or not like mine when I add vanilla pecan ice cream onto a grocery list.

People who don't pursue writing need a simple boost in confidence. How do you increase your confidence? Just write every day and continue to write. I was a student in a creative writing class in our senior center. I've heard a white-haired women say, "When I started, I was a poor writer, but now I'm much better and I'm really proud of myself." Leonardo was an illegitimate child, and on top of that he was a lefty in a world of righties. If those two things didn't stop Leonardo from succeeding, why should a lack of confidence stop you?

Needless to say, writing is enormously important for our civilization. It's humankind's means for communicating—and for collecting and storing information for later dissemination. The systems of graphic marks representing the units of specific languages were invented independently in China, the Near East, and Mesoamerica. Their evolution goes from tokens to pictography, syllabary, and alphabets—which demonstrate the progressive development of dealing with larger and larger amounts of data. When I read that tortoise shells with some sort of symbols carved on them were found in Neolithic graves in China from the seventh millennium BC, I felt sad. Why? I have a tortoise and it pained me to know that her ancestors' carapaces were used for writing on them.

An important form of writing for me is shorthand. I learned Gregg shorthand in high school and later I utilized it for taking notes in college. When I was a substitute teacher, instead of teaching a subject like algebra which I knew nothing about, I had no trouble maintaining discipline when I taught the students how to write their names in shorthand. I also worked in private schools and taught shorthand. One of the business schools was in the basement of the Empire State Building. Shorthand can be a useful secret language.

CHAPTER 2

Tools

A PLUMBER NEEDS a plunger; a carpenter, a saw; and a tailor, a sewing machine. A writer needs different kinds of tools. It doesn't take much to write—a pencil or a pen, and a ream of paper, the inexpensive kind. Why waste money on expensive paper when you're going to rewrite and rewrite what you have written before?

I started making wiggly lines with crayons while I was still in diapers. When I entered the first grade, I was presented by my parents with the gift of a pencil box that contained pencils and a pencil sharpener. I was thrilled with my present and guarded it day and night. What was so advantageous was the eraser at the tip. I erased a lot. Erasers are good for building confidence.

It's just recently that I learned about the history of pencils. At one time I did wonder if Adam and Eve used pencils to send love letters to each other, but that's pushing history too far.

Actually the history of the pencil has a dark side. In England in 1564 deposits of graphite were found. This spawned a smuggling industry. I can understand smuggling dope, but graphite? And yet people had a deep desire to write with pencils, and I can understand that considering that pens caused smudges and smears.

The pencil industry blossomed when the Cumberland Pencil Company opened in 1832. If you close your eyes, you can imagine a child who was given a pencil of the highest quality composed of graphite that shed no dust and marked paper without those ink blots that looked like the chicken pox. He or she would have done a jig. We have to give credit for the invention to the Aztecs, who had used graphite as markers around the fifteenth century and maybe earlier.

Before I write about the pen, I want to describe my interest in the composition of graphite. It's pure carbon with six carbon atoms that form a ring that slides easily over adjacent rings. Yet, another form of pure carbon is even more interesting to me. If the atomic structure is changed, diamonds are formed. As is said, "Diamonds are a girl's best friend." Frankly, as much as I love pencils, I would rather collect diamonds.

When I advanced to a higher grade in elementary school, I was given a pen. I felt very grownup as I dipped it into the ink well on my desk and proceeded to write. I couldn't control the flow of the ink and many blots appeared. I used blotting paper but that didn't help much. I had wished I could return to writing with pencils.

Neil Gaiman is an English author who writes in notebooks with the Pilot 823 fountain pen made by The Goulet Pen Company. The Pilot 823 sells for around $900, but if you like an inexpensive fountain pen, there's the Jinhao Black Medium that takes cartridges. When you get to the point of autographing your books, you will probably prefer a fountain

 REVA SPIRO LUXENBERG

pen. That's kind of impressive and makes a person feel important. I used to use a pen that lit up when you pressed a button. It also had a choice of three colors. I like one of Neil Gaiman's quotes, "The world always seems brighter when you've just made something that wasn't there before,"—and that can apply to your autographing as well as your output.

When I was in the ninth grade in junior high school, one of the subjects I studied was typing. I've been given many expensive presents in my lifetime, but the one I treasure most was the gift my father brought home for me. It was a used Smith Corona typewriter. I don't know if I would have written books with a pen if I hadn't practiced typing on my Smith Corona. It certainly helped me during my college years. During the summers I was in Brooklyn College I worked as a typist and earned enough money to pay for books and clothes.

When I was an adult and needed to work, I taught typing—but that's a long story that I won't go into at this point. The knowledge of typing has paid off well in my life. My sons and my husband both type well with the hunt-and-peck method, but they would have saved time and effort by learning to type with all nine fingers. The left thumb is never used.

After World War II when I was in Brooklyn College, ballpoint pens became the writing instrument in demand. They have existed since the late nineteenth century. Marcel Bich introduced them to Americans in the 1950's. He shortened his name to Bic in 1953—my husband thinks it's not hard to guess why, but I won't go there—and his inexpensive pens took off. The ballpoint pen relies on gravity to coat the ball with ink. There are now, unlike standard ballpoints, pens that write underwater and upside-down. I don't swim and I will never be an astronaut, so this doesn't apply to me.

If you have dreams of being published, you really need to master the computer. I started out, however, with a word processor that I bought in a small store in New Castle, Pennsylvania. My neighbor told me that it was easier to use a computer than a word processor. I had gone back to the store so many times to ask questions about how to use the machine that the owner said, "I don't want to sell you a computer. You'll never learn how to use it." By this time I had decided to go to a ten-day-long writing workshop. So I bought a laptop and a miniature printer and brought them with me.

The workshop took place in a majestic home in Connecticut. I was completely lost, not even knowing how to turn the darn machine on. As for the composing, I didn't know how to double space or paginate. I kept begging peers there for help. I was lucky they didn't beat me up or force me out.

The way plumbers need tools writers need reference books. I bought *Merriam-Webster's Collegiate Dictionary, Roget's Super Thesaurus, Glazier's Word Menu,* and *The Chicago Manual of Style.* With a dictionary you can check the meaning of words and their spelling. It also has foreign words and phrases. Other useful information is included like documentation of sources, footnotes and endnotes, and the form of address for the president of the U.S. Every once in a while there's an illustration and photographs of a word. I like to look at them.

The thesaurus is invaluable for synonyms and antonyms. For instance, take the word "beautiful." You can substitute for

     REVA SPIRO LUXENBERG

that "attractive," "pretty," "handsome," "becoming," "comely" (I like that one), "fair," "lovely," "good-looking," "nice," "gorgeous," "captivating." For the word "excellent," you'll find "great," "fantastic," "superb," "splendid," or "superior."

There are times you may need the opposite meaning— like "ugly," "unattractive," "homely," "repulsive," "awful," "terrible," or "rotten."

Another convincing example is "beer" which you can call "lager," "malt," "bitter," "suds," "stout," "cold one," "brew," "brewski," "Clydesdale piss," *(very colorful)* or "panther piss." Under "beer" is the heading, Word Find and listed is "cask," "keg," "puncheon," "tun," "cup/glass," "mug," "stein," "toby," "schooner," "foam:" "head," "froth," "bead," "Ingredients": "hops," "malt (mash)," "yeast", Manufacturer: "brewery." Now if you're not befuddled or intoxicated, inebriated, and under the weather, go out right now and get yourself a helpful thesaurus.

Random House Webster's Word Menu is an indispensable source for writers. This is a lexical reference book organized by subject material. For example I needed another word for "walk" when I was writing *The Beauty School Murder.* One of my characters is Rhajmah, an Indian lady who walks into the grocery. I didn't want to write "At 8:15 a.m. Rhajmah walked into the grocery." I consulted the book and changed "walked" to "glided." It sounded so much better. I could see her gliding into the grocery dressed in her sari so I wrote, "At 8:15 a.m. Rhajmah glided into the grocery." Under "Verbs of Motion" I found "Gaits" and under "Gaits" there are approximately seventy-one words dealing with movement. To me that's amazing. I've turned to *Word Menu* thousands of times when I wrote my books.

It's important to be consistent in writing and when you need a recognized book of style, turn to *The Chicago Manual of Style*. I would have preferred a Brooklyn analogue since I spent my childhood and most of my adulthood in Brooklyn, but Chicago is in the title and that book will have to do. It is a definitive work and if you and your husband don't agree on how to write a number, the book solves the problem and you won't have to consult a lawyer about a divorce.

The Chicago Manual of Style states the rule about writing numbers as "whole numbers from one through one hundred, round numbers, and any number beginning a sentence" are spelled out. For example instead of writing "a three hundred pound woman in a tent-like dress," you write "a 300 pound woman in a tent-like dress."

You don't have to buy these books new. I bought a used copy of *The Chicago Manual of Style* for an unbelievably low price.

Sometimes I like to quote sayings or authors and I use another reference book *The Describer's Dictionary, A Treasury of Terms & Literary Quotations* by David Grambs & Ellen S. Levine.

Another book that's useful is the Bible, which is good for titles or clever sayings. It's a no-brainer where I got my book title *And There Was Light*.

I know nothing about baseball but when I needed a guide, I turned to *How to Speak Baseball* by James Charlton and Sally Cook. The book has hilarious illustrations.

 REVA SPIRO LUXENBERG

Sometimes I forget what books I own and I buy the same one again. For example, I had the *NTC's Super-Mini American Slang Dictionary.* The book is portable, concise, and has helpful dialogue. A couple of years later I purchased *American Slang,* edited by Barbara Ann Kipfer and Robert Chapman. My knowledge of slang is limited, and these books have helped me jazz up my dialogues.

I own *The Describer's Dictionary* by David Grambs and Ellen S. Levine. The literary quotations are written in block paragraphs. It does have a considerable treasury of terms. So far I haven't used this book. I think it will come in handy one day.

A Writer's Reference by Diana Hacker is particularly useful since the book lies flat and has ten section dividers that provide important organization. The sections are "Composing and revising," "Effective sentences," "Word choice," "Grammatical sentences," "ESL trouble spots," "Punctuation," "Mechanics," "Research writing," "Documentation," and "Basic grammar." "ESL" refers to learners of English as a second language. The correct term now is "ESOL" for "English for Speakers of Other Languages," which accords more respect to the diverse learners.

Finally, if you are writing a mystery, you may need *Deadly Doses: A Writer's Guide to Poisons* by Serita Deborah Stevens and Anne Klarner. I think most writers don't have any knowledge of poisons, with the exception of Agatha Christie who worked in a hospital pharmacy during World War I. I used the toxin of the poison-dart frog in my book *The Beauty School Murder,* but I learned about it from a newspaper article, not from this book which, as a matter of fact, doesn't list it—perhaps because a toxin is mostly described as a drug produced by microorganisms.

A valuable tool for mystery writers is *Police Procedure & Investigation* by Lee Lofland. If you decide to follow in the footsteps of the author Patricia D. Cornwell whose protagonist is Kay Scarpetta, a chief medical examiner, you will find the chapter dealing with autopsy very informative.

I mistakenly bought a second copy of *The Writer's Complete Crime Reference Book* by Martin Roth. It provides the facts on surveillance tactics of the FBI and police and on investigatory and courtroom procedures. The information provided in this book can help you add authenticity and credibility to your story. You want readers to believe that you really know what you're talking about.

Okay, now say you are well into writing your mystery and need help. The book *Writing and Selling Your Mystery Novel* by Hallie Ephron is a comprehensive guide. The last three chapters deal with selling your book and may come in handy. Not only is this work useful, it's fun to read because the author injects humor.

CHAPTER 3

Space

HOW I WISH I had a room with a door for my space! My husband writes in a bedroom which he uses as his office. I'm writing in a corner of the living room. When I'm there concentrating and in the middle of a sentence, my husband interrupts, "I just got an e-mail from Jack. He and Ann want to have lunch with us tomorrow. What should I answer him?" When this happens, I get so irritated that my mind goes as blank as an empty sheet of paper.

Virginia Woolf gave this well-known advice, "A woman must have money and a room of her own if she is going to write." How true.

When I was in Gary Provost's ten-day writers' workshop, he provided a sign for all participants, "DO NOT DISTURB. WRITER AT WORK."

Unfortunately I don't have a door. The dining area and kitchen are adjacent to my working area. I have communicated to my husband that I need privacy. It's not his fault when he interrupts. Sometimes he's impulsive and gets so excited by news that he bursts out like a shock wave. He's a person who can't postpone sharing news. He's wonderful but . . . .

I hope you have a room with a door. Another distraction may be a pet. When I had my lovable cat Fluffy, she wanted attention so much she would jump up on my desk and put her paw on my keyboard. I had to remove her to another part of the house.

On the cover of Stephen King's book *On Writing* is his picture at work. I don't envy the fact he sells as many books as stars in the sky. But I do envy his private nook, his tools spread around his space, and his having a quiet dog. King is sitting in a comfortable desk chair, leaning back in the chair with his long legs stretched out and crossed on his desk. He's writing on a pad in privacy, alone except for the photographer who took that picture.

My desk has two built-in file cabinets that I absolutely need. My space includes reference books, notebooks, and paper. I made room in an adjoining bookcase for ink cartridges for my printer.

I have access to my wireless phone which I keep in a corner of my desk. Its sharp ring is an interruption that can't be avoided in this technological age. However, there's something I do to minimize the disturbance. If I find that it's someone in my family or circle of friends, I do stop what I'm doing and talk. If it's a telemarketer, sometimes I say, "Thank you, but I have no time to talk to you." You don't have to feel guilty if you hang up almost immediately and then get back to work. Have I mentioned that writing is work? Well, it is.

I used to keep phone numbers in a phone directory. When I found that a number had lost its usefulness, I crossed it out. I discovered that for me the best way to record names, landline and cell phone numbers, fax numbers, and e-mail addresses is

　　　REVA SPIRO LUXENBERG

to put them in a Rolodex. When I don't need the information any more, I extract the card and drop it in the waste paper basket. By the way a waste paper basket in my writing area is useful. A shredder is another device that provides peace of mind.

I attend a ceramics class and have painted many beautiful and useful pieces for my L-shaped desk. A colorful pitcher holds markers; a vase, pencils and calligraphy pens; and a mug with the image of an old-time sailor, pens. The head of an owl is another ceramic piece. It has a curved nose on which my reading glasses rest.

Sometimes when the air-conditioner turns on, I sneeze and don't have to go far to reach for a tissue in a holder shaped like three piled-up leather books.

I also have a separate book for passwords. Without it, to keep them together, I would lose my mind.

In a small file cabinet on my desk there are the identifying cards that people freely give out.

Every writer should have his or her address cards. Mine have a picture of books with my name, the word "AUTHOR" underneath, and my particulars below that. I keep some of these cards in a card holder on my desk, some in my purse, and some in a box in another desk drawer.

I almost overlooked something very important, my stapler.

My desk drawers, I must admit, are cluttered—but with items that are necessary for a writer: like scissors, address labels, staples, scotch tape, rubber bands, a box of paper clips, and small notebooks. (Would you believe that while making this list I just located nail polish in a drawer? It should be in my medicine cabinet.)

The desk drawer to my right contains stamps, a calculator, a camera and charging unit, masking tape, labels, and a box of address cards. That drawer is full; but it's not as crowded as the drawer to my left.

A large artificial plant is in the corner of my desk and a desk lamp lights up my monitor.

There is a tale connected to my gigantic monitor. My younger son accompanied me to the store when I bought it. It measures thirty-two inches diagonally. The following is what transpired between my son Allen and me at the time.

"This is just the kind of monitor you need, Mom."

"It's awfully big."

"It'll fit on your desk and you'll love it."

My son can be very persuasive, so I bought it. Afterwards I learned what was in his mind. He thought that because the monitor was so large I wouldn't have to wear my reading glasses. He was wrong. I still had to wear them. I got used to that monitor anyway, and now I wouldn't trade it in for a smaller one.

I bought a desktop computer and a week later lightning hit it and it went caput, so I bought another one. Since then I've gone through many, but I must say I'd still rather use a desktop than a laptop. I had pain in my shoulder and a doctor advised me to get a split keyboard—which I did. It's really an ergonomic keyboard that minimizes muscle strain. It's a single board, with the keys separated into two groups at a different angle from the typical straight keyboard. I follow doctor's orders except for exercising. It took me a week to get used to the split keyboard, but it's a wonderful invention, and I won't part with it from now on.

     REVA SPIRO LUXENBERG

Although I had been hounded to upgrade to Word 10, I resisted and I'm still using Word 8. When you're my age, it's hard to adapt to anything new. My cell phone, in fact, doesn't have texting.

I have a wireless phone on the desk that is a source of interruption, but at least I don't have to get up and run to the kitchen to answer it.

CHAPTER 4

Health

IF ON SOME days, like when I have a cold, I can't write, I feel deprived . . . I feel guilty . . . I yearn to sit at my computer and perform my daily routine.

Writing takes strength and so I eat to fuel my brain. I try to consume protein, fruits, vegetables, and nuts. I go to sleep at the same time every night and I work with renewed energy in the morning. Other people work better at night like my husband who often writes at 3 a.m. when I'm fast asleep. Sometimes he pretends to write, but he really plays Spider Solitaire or reads the digital edition of *The New York Times* on his computer. I'm really revealing family secrets, aren't I?

Sleep is important for a creative mind. I usually get into bed at 8 p.m. After saying my prayers I write whatever pops into my mind—a few sentences—in my journal which is a succession of small notebooks. My journal won't be published—at least it better not be—it's for my use and mine alone. When I finish a notebook, I reread it and I'm surprised that I have forgotten many things that happened during the period it has covered.

I have a lamp that attaches to my bedpost and I spend time reading all kinds of books.

In the morning, after my shower, I grab hold of *642 Things to Write About* and I finish one prompt. While I'm drying off and dressing, I listen to music on a cassette player and I sing along. I consider all these activities and routines as contributing to my physical and emotional health. They, in fact, sustain my writing.

My television watching is limited basically to current news, but I do love the reruns of Star Trek. I find the episodes mature and creative.

Exercise is another component of health. I do the basics, which, as I suggested, is "less than the doctor ordered." I like to walk in the pool. I like to imagine that I exercise my fingers when I use my computer. This puts "sound mind" before "sound body," which I know is a pretense.

Writing is a lonely task, so for mental health I reach out to family, friends, and doctors. Sometimes when I have an appointment with a physician, I bring one of my books as a gift. He or she appreciates it and it makes for good rapport. I have said it's important for a writer to read. When I'm not seen on time, I read a book I've brought to the waiting room and I spend the downtime proactively.

As I have said, things that make me happy contribute to my mental health. Since my time is limited, as is everyone's, I have had to eliminate some activities like painting with acrylics, quilting, and sewing clothes. I do look forward to my weekly ceramics group. I love to go shopping, but this takes time so I have been, increasingly, buying stuff on the Internet.

I enjoy taking care of my Testudo tortoise, Mordy.

I don't know if there is such a thing as perfect health but I'm determined to be as healthy as I can—without being compulsive about following the doctor's instructions.

According to Walter Isaacson's biography on *Leonardo da Vinci*, Leonardo used to carry small notebooks wherever he went and jot down ideas. He filled pages of his notebooks with thoughts, drawings, and descriptions. Isaacson quoted one of Leonardo's writings, "Medicines, when properly used, restore health to invalids, and a doctor will make the right use of them if he understands the nature of man." Even this great genius was concerned with health.

CHAPTER 5

Planning

I DON'T THINK a writer's planning a novel too far ahead is helpful. I remember once when I left a writing conference I offered a fellow participant, who had come by bus, a lift home in my car. It was a long ride from Bristol, Connecticut, to her residence in Manhattan. During the three hours of the trip she attempted to plot a novel. She kept changing her mind and made me miserable. This isn't to say that there aren't people who do this successfully. I'm not one of them. I'm not a good chess player, you see, because I can't anticipate future moves. Gradually I get to know my characters and how they react when faced with problems and their problems become the plot.

Try both ways and see which one suits you.

When I begin my novel with a character faced with a problem, I don't have to imagine the rest to begin writing the draft. I find that not knowing what's coming next stimulates my imagination and keeps my interest piqued. If I can picture my protagonist with her particular personality, she will lead me.

Many times I don't know the end of the book in advance and I surprise myself. This happened in *The Bumbling Bigamist.* I won't give the ending away, but it really is a bombshell. It dawned on me much later than you would believe. It happened when I was writing the very last chapter.

Speaking about ideas, I often ask myself what I should write about. I can ponder about a topic for a minute or several years. Agatha Christie wrote in her book *Agatha Christie: An Autobiography,* "It is an odd feeling to have a book growing inside you, for perhaps six or seven years. . . ."

The biography written by Rudolf Schrock and published in Germany about the secret double life of Charles A. Lindbergh inspired me to write *The Bumbling Bigamist.* Lindbergh had three families and seven children in Europe in addition to his American family back home. Wow! I thought it would be interesting to write a mystery about a bigamist. I wouldn't of course make him famous like Lindbergh, who became a national icon with his nonstop solo flight across the Atlantic in 1927 in his single-engine plane. Actually I was amazed when I saw the plane "The Spirit of St. Louis" hanging in the Smithsonian National Air and Space Museum in Washington, D.C. The plane was very small. How did he do it? I also recalled how in 1932 tragedy came to Lindbergh and his wife when his twenty-month-old son was kidnapped and murdered.

I don't remember how I came to write *The Cereal Killer* about a serial killer who sprinkles cereal on the bodies of his victims. I do know that one of my writing friends had said it was a terrible idea as she attempted to discourage me. The story had percolated in my mind. I wrote it piecemeal until I

     REVA SPIRO LUXENBERG

finished it after thirteen years. I sure am glad I hadn't let my friend dissuade me.

Ideas may sprout from anywhere. I was teaching sewing to junior high school students when, with dismay, I looked at the blackboard where I had written directions. I was ashamed of my scraggly handwriting. I then took out calligraphy books from the library and created a new easy way to write calligraphy. It took me three weeks to come up with a new way to write each letter. After I had perfected fifty-two letters and numbers from one to ten, I published *Romantic Calligraphy*.

Unusual circumstances prompted me to write *Murder at the Second Lily Pond*. I was retired and living in Scottsdale, Arizona, when I made plans to fly to a three-day writing conference in Oxford, England. I planned to explore England and travel on to Swansea, Wales, to observe a school that teaches the making of stained glass. I took the first British Airways flight from Phoenix. With the delays at the airport it took eleven hours before we landed. I was exhausted, and as I usually do, I made my way to the restroom before going through customs. The official there asked to see my passport and I searched in my purse and pockets for it in vain.

"I'm sorry," I said contritely. "I don't know what happened to my passport. Will you send me back to Phoenix?" I might have panicked if I had not been so exhausted.

"No, we'll search the plane," he said.

Five minutes later a woman waved her hand in my direction. "I found this passport in the bathroom," she said.

What a relief!

The next mishap happened when I was directed to the railroad station. I had one suitcase and as I descended the staircase, a stranger grabbed it. *Oh, my God, he's going to steal my stuff.* But he didn't. He was just a good Samaritan who wanted to help me.

Many trains were lined up in the station. I approached an official, "Please tell me which train is bound for Oxford?" He pointed to one. I boarded it and wearily sat down. An hour later I was asked for my ticket. I held it out. "Sorry, madam," the Englishman said. "You're on the wrong train."

I had to go back to the station and board the right train to Oxford. Unbelievable!

When I got there, I took a taxi to St. Francis College and was shown my room. It was spartan. I had bought some picture postcards of castles in England and I attached them with masking tape to the walls. I need pretty pictures to look at. That's just me.

Though it was August, the weather was cold and dreary with pouring rain. My arthritic back started to hurt. A fellow participant suggested I take a bath to ease my muscles.

"I haven't taken a bath in about forty years," I said. "I always take showers."

"Here are some bath salts," she said. "I'll wait outside the door until you come out."

"Thanks for your concern and generosity."

The three-day conference was very stimulating and everyone was very friendly. I was happy I had come. I asked one British author about my intended murder mystery, "How many victims do you think I should have?"

"Not too many," he said. "My books are set in India," he continued, "The advice given to writers, you know, is to write about a familiar location. But I've never actually been

     REVA SPIRO LUXENBERG

to India. I've researched everything. Would you care for some sherry?"

He handed me a glass with sherry. I sipped it. It was not to my taste. I like sweet wine.

Three days later I walked into the American Express office. "Please cancel my other trips."

The American Express clerk was gracious and did as I asked. "I have a bad case of arthritis," I said. "Please book me for a trip back to Phoenix."

She did. "That will be £1500."

"What?" I exclaimed. "Why that's about $3,000. I can't afford that. I'll stay in Oxford. Please check me into a hotel."

I took a taxi to the hotel. They had no elevator. "We have a room with a bath on the third floor," the clerk said.

"I have arthritic knees. I can't climb steps."

"We have a room on the ground floor without a bath."

I took it. The weather changed considerably. It became humid and hot. There was no air conditioning and I needed a shampoo.

My delay in Oxford, strange as it might seem, influenced me. I decided I would set my mystery in Oxford. I went to the local library. "Where is your restroom?"

"We have no restroom. If you go across the street to the department store, you'll find the restroom up one flight."

I had no choice. When I entered the department store, I discovered that the first floor featured cosmetics and jewelry. That cost me plenty as I can't pass by such displays without buying something. I also had my hair shampooed in the beauty parlor.

Now I had to decide where in Oxford I should set my mystery. I didn't yet know who was going to be murdered, or who would solve the murder, but I first needed a quiet spot for the foul play. I couldn't put it in a typical Oxford home, as I had never been in one.

I took a taxi to the Botanic Garden and began walking around when I spotted a young woman on her knees weeding a garden plot. "Excuse me. I'm looking for a quiet place for a murder," I said.

The young woman, more startled than puzzled—and somewhat alarmed as well—jumped up and stared at me.

"I'm a writer," I said, "and I need to find a deserted area."

The young woman smiled. "You frightened me, you know. My first thought was that you were an American loony who wanted to do me in!"

"Terribly sorry," I said.

She continued, "If you walk down this path, you'll come to the second lily pond. Usually people don't go that far. Good luck!"

When I found the second lily pond, I took numerous photos of it. I located the murder there and entitled the mystery *Murder at the Second Lily Pond.*

CHAPTER 6

Working Habits

I DO TAKE one day off per week from writing, but I want to stress that, other than that break, it's important to work at a steady pace. By my following this rule I keep my memory fresh.

Journal writing is the easiest form of writing except for making shopping lists. I note one or two things that are on my mind, such as how I feel about what had happened that day. I may or may not search for metaphors that express what things feel like. It depends how tired I am.

I date the journal from the initial date until the latest one. My journal is a series of notebooks in which I record anything that seems important at the time. Once my husband needed a fact about a conversation that had taken place months before and I found it for him.

I try not to block my flow of thoughts by being too self-critical. When I'm depressed or hurting, I note more facts than feelings, but I do mention my anxieties.

When I first started keeping a journal, I bought some types that weren't wirebound. I later found that a wire binding helps the book lie flat. I also like journals that have an elastic band attached to the back cover for going back to the exact spot I left off.

There are journals of all types and prices in the market. Some have metallic covers; others come in genuine handmade leather or leatherette. One attractive journal has a cover with a magnetic clasp. There are writing-prompt journals. I've seen one with a cover in laser- cut wood. Some are unlined. I prefer lined.

I like journals with pictures of dogs, birds, or butterflies on the cover.

Journaling whets my writing appetite. It's like having an entrée before the meal.

* * *

It's very annoying when I want to print what I have written and the ink in the cartridge is running out, just like when I need ketchup and it isn't there. To anticipate this situation, as I've pointed out earlier, I buy a few cartridges ahead of time.

I used to have an expensive printer that made me gnash my teeth. I had the hardest time changing the cartridge. It got to a point that I donated it to charity with an apology. I then bought an inexpensive printer that runs like a top. It warns me when I should consider changing the ink. After the warning I usually get about ten more pages until the cartridge runs out of ink.

* * *

 REVA SPIRO LUXENBERG

I used to be lazy about looking up unfamiliar words in the dictionary, but I'm much better about that now. After all the larger my vocabulary the better my writing.

* * *

The time of day that I write is important. I have the most energy in the morning. That isn't to say that you may not do better in the middle of the night. As I said before, that's when my husband does his best work, and that's when I'm in dreamland. To each his own.

I read an interesting article written by Kristen Bahler in the December 2017 issue of *Money* magazine entitled "Go Ahead—Press the Snooze Button: Waking up early doesn't make you more productive." Her conclusion is that according to a growing body of research what really counts is being consistent. She mentions three studies that stress that the more variable one's sleep schedule is the worse the results are.

* * *

What really disturbs me is being interrupted. I have two maids who are very pleasant and funny, but who make noise when they're cleaning. As long as they do their thing, however, I can do mine. In fact, I believe I write more when they're present than otherwise. Even the noise of the vacuum doesn't disturb me.

* * *

If you're looking for ideas for short stories or novels, it's helpful to subscribe to magazines in different fields. I don't spend much time reading newspapers but you may prefer to. I do watch the news on various channels on TV. Ideas spring up when you least expect them. I find the Internet invaluable for research. Sometimes I do need to go to my local library to dig deeper into what I'm investigating.

* * *

How many words do I write each day? That depends. Sometimes I can write only a paragraph; other times I'm completely satisfied when I write a thousand words. Microsoft Word gives me a feeling of accomplishment by keeping track of my accruing word total.

I've found that when I'm hungry I can't write—not a sentence, not a word, not even a letter. I'm close to the kitchen and I have a satisfying nosh like fruit yogurt or a bagel with butter. Afterwards I return to my computer.

* * *

It's pleasurable to have a wireless mouse that doesn't require my feeding it cheese for it to function.

* * *

I've already indicated that nighttime isn't my best time for writing. When I'm tired, I can't write. My mentor Gary Provost wrote in *100 Ways to Improve Your Writing,* "Use your own common sense." If my eyes are burning and my head is drooping, I realize it's time to say goodnight to my computer.

 REVA SPIRO LUXENBERG

CHAPTER 7

Writing Tips

I PAY CLOSE attention to an author's style when I read. Style is the form in which an idea is expressed. You'll sense why the author chose a word or why she formulated two short sentences instead of one long one. You become aware of other choices a writer makes. You needn't adopt the particular author's style. After you have written a while, you'll develop your own style. You want to sound like you, not like anyone else.

I also list phrases under *Vocabulary* in a separate file on my computer. I like action verbs that don't need adverbs to drag them down.

I make an effort to come up with my own metaphors. That takes thought. It's worth it. Clichés, however, though clever, should be avoided. An exception is when a character uses one in a dialogue.

There are lists of the most commonly misspelled words. Study them. A misspelled word will jar a reader and wreck your credibility. I find that *Word* on my computer attempts to change my spelling. For example, I'll write "its," and it will *change* it to "it's." Actually, as a case in point, it just put a blue line under both. When the program turns "it's" to "it," I don't grimace. I just say, "You don't know what you're doing." To test Word's capacities I once purposely wrote "ocasionally" with one "c" and it added the additional one.

The opening sentence of an article, story, or novel should be provocative. You thus create an anticipation that something interesting is coming. This lead takes your readers into your story so that they won't close your book on the spot never to open it again.

Set a mood and stick with it. If you write a humorous book, it should contain humor throughout.

Have an editor review your work. My husband is an excellent editor. Besides, he doesn't charge me. Of course, in exchange I serve him tasty nutritious home-cooked meals. Also I listen to his stories even when he's not as concise as he should be.

When I write a novel, I keep in mind Jane Austen's quotation, "If a book is well written, I always find it too short." I keep the reader in mind and try to make it as interesting as I can. A lot depends upon the character of the protagonist, the star of the book who has a problem to solve.

If you're writing a novel, you may wonder if you should create a protagonist based on yourself. If the protagonist is you, you have a dilemma because it's tough to view yourself objectively. You may incorporate aspects of your experience in the setting and characterization as I did in *Grand Army Plaza*—my familiarity with libraries and my background as a school social worker.

You may base your characters in part on real people, but only "in part." You don't want your brother-in-law to sue

  REVA SPIRO LUXENBERG

you. Besides, if you use Irving exactly as he is, you'll limit your imagination. I think of fiction as similar to lying. You would do well to take a trait from your daughter, who is a well-controlled neat freak, and combine it with something of Aunt Bessie, who is quick-tempered and messy.

There's another way to approach selecting characters and that is to use people you don't know like someone in the newspaper or a distant acquaintance. Ideas fly in from all over. Just write something that stirs your imagination.

Writing short paragraphs is faster and livelier. I like white space when I read. It's not often I write a long paragraph. I do that only when I find it necessary to expand a pertinent idea.

New writers tend to write dialogue between two people in one paragraph. That's a no-no. Every time a person speaks, you need a new paragraph. To write dialogue that sounds real, be sure to mimic spoken language. When your character has a regional speaking manner, I think it's important not to emphasize it constantly. Every once in a while you may remind the reader that the person speaks with a southern accent. For instance, "Why don't y'all come into the dining room?"

In the *Writer's Digest*, March/April 2018, there's an article by D. L. Podlesni which included thoughts about characters with accents. She stresses that a writer should ask whether a character needs an accent. If you do choose to use an accent, then research it and apply it with subtlety.

I used an Indian accent for my character Rhajmah. When I read what I had written to my writing group, they said, "Get rid of the accent," so I did. I didn't want to turn her into a stereotype.

Strong titles are important for books. *"Gone with the Wind,"* Margaret Mitchell's is a memorable one. The author considered various titles until she settled on phrases written in the book itself, as when Scarlett muses, "Was Tara still standing or was Tara also gone with the wind which had swept through Georgia?" At first she had come up with *"Tomorrow Is Another Day,"* the last line of the novel, which in my opinion makes a good title. She also considered *"Bugles Sang True."* I don't care for that one. Another title she had in mind was *"Not in Our Stars,"* which makes sense. The title *"Gone with the Wind"* is both about losing the South and Scarlett losing Rhett Butler. It also comes from a poem by Emily Dickinson, *"Sic transit gloria mundi,"* which is translated from Latin as "Thus passes the glory of the world."

Just a short digression about why Margaret Mitchell wrote her Pulitzer Prize-winning novel. She was twenty-five and a journalist for the *Atlanta Journal Sunday Magazine* and had to take a leave of absence to recover from a recurring ankle injury. It was tiresome for her at home, and she, therefore, sought to overcome boredom. It's interesting to note that she spent the next decade working on characters and plot development. She had no intention of publishing the book. So you see you never know how your manuscript can develop.

There are times I spend hours selecting a title. Some people have criticized my titles. One woman in my writing critique group said she didn't like *"An Old Woman's Confessions."* Needless to say, I didn't follow her advice.

The title should make the reader curious. Don't mislead. Be honest. I did think of other titles before I settled on *"The Bumbling Bigamist,"* which obviously is a mystery about a bigamist. I liked the alliteration. A good title is short. You needn't give away the plot. Just, if it's possible, have the title suggest something about the content of the story.

To succeed as a writer, you need to avoid grammatical errors. They are fatal. Good writing and good grammar co-exist. The rules of grammar represent organization of the brain's thinking. We need grammatical rules about tense, mood, number, gender, and case. Grammar exists so that people may communicate well. When I'm unsure of something, I consult my husband or, when he's busy writing, I look in *The Chicago Manual of Style.*

Semicolons aren't used as much as they used to be. Now an m-dash has replaced many of them. An m-dash is twice as long as a hyphen. If you have Microsoft Word 8, like I have, check Insert to the right of Home. Symbol then comes up. Look in the symbol section and you'll also find many useful symbols like accent marks. In fact, there are thousands of symbols very many of which you have never even dreamed of.

Commas are my nemesis. There are rules for commas, but I still don't completely understand them. When I think I have inserted a comma correctly, my husband removes it and vice-versa. I used to put a comma in when I took a breath, but that isn't necessarily the right way. Look up the rules in *The Chicago Manual of Style* or marry a man who is proficient in punctuation.

One mistake I find that new writers make is that they change tenses in midstream. They may start in the present tense and switch to the past or vice-versa. This is easy to rectify if you're aware of the need not to do so.

In the historical novel *The Aviator's Wife* by Melanie Benjamin, the author relates how Charles Lindbergh urged his wife Anne to write. She quotes Anne in the first person, "I worked with the myopic concentration of an artisan: I would not be hurried." She couldn't adopt her husband's suggestion that she set a schedule for a certain amount of words every day, as he had done; and she took her own time. How many words you write is your decision.

As you begin to write a story or a book, do you picture your reader? My husband writes for highly educated people. I don't do this. For example, when I wrote *An Old Lady's Confessions,* I imagined senior women reading my book. I was surprised when some of the reviews I received on Amazon were from young women who wrote that they benefited from my advice. You can't be sure who will read your book, but in my case when I wrote mysteries, I had in mind that it might be a female mystery-lover.

Think about the educational level of your reader and use suitable language. I keep in mind that my grandchildren are reading my books and I tend to shy away from vulgarity even when it might be appropriate to include it. Sometimes I can't help using an unacceptable word since the story calls for it, but I don't do this often.

There are times to provide statistics to establish your credibility. One man I know wrote about the suicide rate of returning veterans in general terms. It's common knowledge that many veterans come home depressed. I critiqued his piece by saying that he could have improved his admittedly well-written piece with statistics. Too many numbers will numb

       REVA SPIRO LUXENBERG

your reader, but a sprinkling shows you know what you're talking about.

Even though you may be writing fiction, you need to base your information on facts. I had spent five months in Biloxi and heard about Hurricane Camille, but when I wrote *The Bumbling Bigamist*, I needed to research both the hurricane and the geography. I bought a DVD and a book about hurricanes and I utilized the Internet to glean more accurate background information for my fictional work.

I try not to use unnecessary words. They are what are called "redundant." For instance, don't write, "The annual income tax time once a year grates on her nerves." Instead it's better to write, "The annual income tax time grates on her nerves." I read a book I liked called *America's Obsessives: The Compulsive Energy That Built a Nation* by Joshua Kendall. In describing Thomas Jefferson, he stated that the founding father, a voracious reader and a compulsive note taker, once wrote, "The most valuable of all talents is that of never using two words where one will do." I try to emulate Jefferson's example (not that I always succeed). Kendall also wrote about Melvil Dewey, who created the Dewey decimal system for libraries. He wrote that Dewey "preferred 'buyer' to 'purchasing agent'," 'many' to 'a large number of,' and 'invite,' to 'extend an invitation to.'"

Having mentioned Joshua Kendall's book, I'll add something that Charles Lindbergh prided himself on doing, "My record for a single day was 3500 words." I figure if he could endure flying 3,629 miles over the Atlantic from New York to Paris in a tiny plane, it wasn't hard for him to write

3500 words. I certainly won't compare myself to Lindbergh; I'm satisfied when I write a thousand words.

Okay, now I'll tell you what not to do. Don't follow my example. I often make the following mistake, especially in a first draft: I don't keep related words together. Perhaps it's because of the sloppy way I talk. "I loved my teacher Miss Pease, who taught microbiology." Better, "I loved my microbiology teacher Miss Pease."

Parallel construction resembles lines of houses on two sides of a street. It's a way to proceed in a sequence like music does. An example of what not to do is, "Bobby enjoys running, hiking, and to go camping." Parallel construction is, "Bobby enjoys running, hiking, and camping."

When you wish to emphasize words, put them at the end of the sentence. For example, "My name is Reva Spiro Luxenberg and I'm an author." When I put "author" at the end I'm emphasizing my writing. If I wanted to emphasize my name, I would write, "I'm the author Reva Spiro Luxenberg."

"Show, not tell" is an admonition that you hear repeatedly. In my novel *Grand Army Plaza* I could've described a minor character as an old man and left it at that. I chose to write, "He looked like a grandfather with a beanie on his head and a face like a pock-marked English muffin plastered with a milk-white beard."

You may create a character by describing his physical features in detail—or by including his actions, his thoughts, and his words. It's up to you how to present your protagonist.

Minor characters in a narrative receive less attention than a major character, and therefore, just a few details need to be mentioned about them.

Include dialogue to move your story along. A dialogue tag identifies who is speaking, but use these tags sparingly, only when it's impossible to tell who's speaking. In some books I've read I got lost and wondered whether the woman or the man was talking. If there are more than two speakers in a scene, you need to use more dialogue tags. For instance, in one scene in *Murder at the Second Lily Pond* I was dealing with four characters.

> "It's going extremely well," Abraham said.
> "It's a challenge," Jeffrey added.
> "Bully for you. You got it right," Abraham said.
> "Anything that is worthwhile is a challenge."
> Sadie wiped her mouth with her napkin, stood up, and picked up her purse from the sideboard where she had left it. "It's not raining today. Think I'll go out for a breath of fresh air."
> "Where are you going?" Mrs. Bogen asked.

There may be times when you start with a minor fictional character and develop him or her organically as you write. I came to a point in *The Cereal Killer* when I fell in love with my Indian character Rhajmah. I have since used her in all my Sadie Weinstein mysteries. I had never met an Indian woman but I used my imagination and fashioned Rhajmah to be petite, to be addicted to pickles, and most importantly to be a psychic.

I had to give more thought to my major protagonist. She grew like Topsy, a character in Harriet Beecher Stowe's *Uncle Tom's Cabin*. I started Sadie off as a short dark-haired woman in her forties. As she embarked upon her amateur-detective career, she dyed her hair blond. She loved Agatha Christie's mysteries, and she devoted herself to her grocery and to her loyal husband Nathan, who kept warning her to keep out of danger. Not once did she listen to him.

I liked Sadie so much I used her as a character in my story "The Call From Beyond" which was published in *Medley of Murder*, edited by Susan Budavari and Suzanne Flaig. In the story Nathan has died and Sadie is seventy-four. In my imagination time is not a consideration. Sir Arthur Conan Doyle had Sherlock Holmes and I have had Sadie.

Transitional phrases move the reader from one spot to another—either in location or time. The transition should be logical, smooth, and quick. Some transitional phrases are 'the following week,' 'meanwhile, back home,' and 'on the other hand.' In my book *Reflections and Recollections* in the story "Making A Difference," I spoke about teaching in a business school and used the following as a transition, "The time came that I was called into the director's office . . . ."

It's unnecessary to go into detail by describing how George got out of bed, took a shower, brushed his teeth, got dressed, and left the house. Unless something happened to George that was significant, you can skip the details and just tell about how George arrived in the office where he was about to be fired from his job.

Keep on the lookout for metaphors you read in the newspaper. Use a joke you heard on TV. There's a saying that if you steal from one writer, it's called plagiarism, but stealing from several is called research. It's permissible to steal a sentence or a phrase, but if you quote a quantity of lines,

 REVA SPIRO LUXENBERG

you need to get the publisher's permission and give credit to the author.

When you get to the end of your story or novel, stop writing. When the protagonist has solved her problem, quit. Say good-bye and don't linger. In my short story "The Call From Beyond," my last two sentences wind up thus, "I'm going home now," Sadie said with glee. "I'm expecting a long-distance call."

Don't bore your readers. Don't chase them away.

Rewrites are necessary. Resistance is futile! Unless you're a genius with a 300 IQ, you have to go over your work many times. You'll be surprised at how many mistakes you find you correct each time.

CHAPTER 8

Novels

I HADN'T THOUGHT I could write a novel—but I was wrong. I've written four dramas. Some readers said they liked all of them. The books didn't become best sellers, as I wasn't promoting them—in fact very few were sold. One reader rated *Recipe for Love* with five stars and said, "A fast read, sweet story line." I was happy to see this critique on Amazon. I'm pleased I took the time out for writing instead of playing the slot machines in the casino.

Before I started *Recipe for Love,* an idea popped into my head. Greer Garson was an actress who I greatly admired. In the movie *Random Harvest,* she played Paula as the wife of Charles, an amnesiac World War I veteran played by Ronald Coleman. If you haven't seen this movie, I highly recommend it. It has tension and heart. Amnesia is a condition that had fascinated me. I decided to write a book about a woman who has it.

Amnesia may also be worked into a comedy, like the movie *Overboard* starring Goldie Hawn, who is living a life of luxury with her husband when she falls off their yacht, gets a blow on the head, and forgets everything. A widowed carpenter with four kids claims she's his wife and turns her into a working-class mother of four.

I was inspired to write *A Flickering Flame,* as I was intrigued by the psychological condition of *pseudologia fantastica,* a behavior of habitual or compulsive lying. It was first described in 1891 by Anton Delbrueck in the medical literature. It's listed in the *DSM,* that is *The Diagnostic and Statistical Manual of Medical Disorders.* One of my grandsons urged me to tell a tale about a man who had this rare condition. Psychology has always interested me since I had been a psychiatric social worker. The review on Amazon—which, of course, I like—was "A very exciting story! A must read!"

You use the incidents from your life to make them happen to a character who isn't you. Chaya Bloom in my drama *Grand Army Plaza* is a caring, lovable protagonist. I like to think I possess these qualities, but Chaya goes to great lengths by adopting a child of another religion and color, which I myself might not do. I admire her greatly and that is evident in my novel.

You may wonder how I came to write that book. There's a simple answer. When at the end of the day when I was a school social worker and I was leaving my intermediate school to go home, I encountered a woman at the door. "I'm Mrs. Luxenberg, the social worker," I said to her. "May I help you?"

"No thank you," she answered. "I'm waiting for my son."

There were only African American students in the entire school and I wondered how this Caucasian woman happened to be there. I guess I looked puzzled because she explained, "My neighbor was black and she knew she was dying. She had no relatives so she asked me to care for her son and I did.

Since he's small, I need to protect him by walking him to and from school."

At that moment her son, a boy of short stature with a shy smile, appeared. I watched them as they walked away together. *What a wonderful thing for a woman to do.*

I admired her so much that years later I expanded her character by giving her a history, a family, and deep religious convictions. I gave her big problems to solve. Then with this imaginary character in an interesting plot I completed a screen play. When it wasn't accepted, I turned it into a novel. A review on Amazon that pleased me the most was, "This book is a heart-warming gem."

My stimulus for writing *And There Was Light* came from a woman I knew who had an operation by a surgeon who was unaware he was using a contaminated cystoscope. The woman, as a result, had to be tested for Hepatitis and HIV AIDS for six months. I worked this into the story. Praise of a reader on Amazon was "I enjoyed the book from cover to cover."

There's no single way to write a novel. Helen Fielding wrote a fictitious diary in first person, *Bridget Jones's Diary,* described by *USA TODAY* as "Screamingly funny!"

You're free to do it your way. You can outline in advance or not. You can start writing in your sixties, seventies, eighties, or nineties. I'm not so sure about starting when you hit one hundred, but I don't think it's impossible. Your brain may work like a well-greased motor even then. You can write any time or any place you want. You can sit or you can imitate Hemingway and write standing up.

 REVA SPIRO LUXENBERG

Be satisfied with whatever amount of words you put on paper each day whatever your individual pace. I get very excited when I see that I've written a thousand words. I'm an old lady and I tire easily, so I do stop at that number feeling satisfied and at peace.

The size of a novel is from 80,000 to over a 100,000 words so if you really like the characters, the plot, and the theme, stick with it. When you start out, think about what matters in the lives of your characters. They have to want something that isn't easy to get. For instance, let's say you want to write about a man who has lost his wife and falls in love again. You could say "Roger met Patricia and they dated for a year. They fell in love and they got married." How dull! There have to be obstacles to their romance or you don't have a story. What kind of obstacles? All kinds—like they live in different cities, Patricia is engaged to someone else, Roger has ten children and Patricia doesn't want to care for such a large family.

The obstacles have to get progressively more difficult before they are resolved at the end. Make it hard for the main characters to accomplish what they really care about.

Different genres involve different expectations of length and subject matter. You need to clarify whether you're writing a romance, a fantasy, science fiction, a sedate mystery, or a thriller. Before you start, you should research the parameters.

Bookstores have sections that are arranged by genre. Readers know what they're looking for when they browse; they're often searching for something in particular. Your book should not overlap genres, especially if you're a new writer. By choosing the genre you will save yourself time-consuming revisions. However, if you choose to work on a multi-genre collection, that's up to you.

If you want to write that romance, there is one thing you need to do before you start—to format your manuscript. Agents and publishers expect you to follow basic formatting steps. Ignore this suggestion if you are writing only for the eyes of your family or friends, or only for yourself. But I think there's another thing you should consider in advance. Don't sell yourself short and underestimate the appeal that your book might have for wider and wider audiences.

The manuscript should be double-spaced with one-inch margins. Each paragraph should be indented. Number the pages. In other words the page numbers shouldn't restart with every new chapter which I once encountered in a manuscript that I was editing.

Number your chapters. A warning—be careful with this as I have made mistakes in some books by giving the same number to two respective chapters. Don't do what I did—do as I say.

When I first learned to type, I used two spaces after periods. We no longer do this. It's one space and only one space.

Be extremely careful about backing up your work besides saving it periodically. Saving is manual; backing up is programmed on scheduled intervals. Soon after I moved to Florida, my computer was damaged by an electrical storm, but since I had a Carbonite backup drive, I was able to retrieve my work. There are a number of different backup programs you can install.

 REVA SPIRO LUXENBERG

Suppose you read *The New York Times* on Sunday and you notice that many novels deal with the office of President of the U.S. You think *Ah, ha, I'll write a book about a fictitious senator who runs for President and gets himself into trouble. It'll be easier to get published.* Forget that. You have devoted a year writing an interesting book, hunted nine months for an agent, and waited a year for your agent to succeed with a publisher—but by now the market is featuring science fiction. The public is clamoring for science fiction and you've wasted years of your precious life. Be wary of trends like you avoid high calorie desserts. If you have a "sweet tooth," that's not a good example.

You decide you're going to write an original novel, but your ideas aren't so hotsy-totsy. You can overcome frustration by telling a familiar story in an unconventional way. You select another location and another time. You create original characters and tell your story in a unique style. Start with something fresh, because if you don't, your readers will say they had heard this story before and relegate your book to the garbage pail. You certainly don't want that.

You need a plot. I consider this the hardest part of writing a novel. It can be done by coming up with an unusual premise, taking the protagonist on a quest, and having her face several challenges. Aristotle invented this approach, which is named the "Aristotelian Arc" after him. Something happens to your protagonist's life to upset it. She wants something. She goes on a journey—physical or spiritual—to get what she wants. She encounters obstacles of increasing complexity and intensity. At the end either she gets what she wants or she doesn't, but she ends up a changed person.

I'm not telling you how to write literary fiction, but you should be aware that the plot tends to develop subliminally via the thoughts and decisions of the characters. Literary fiction is often more nerve-wracking to read, and it certainly is difficult to write. I have never tried it. If you have the motivation and the stamina, go ahead. Your novel may be a masterpiece.

I suggest you keep a list of your characters' names and physical characteristics. I have come to the middle of a book and have forgotten what color eyes my protagonist has. I have to go back and see how I've described her.

As I pointed out, a novel has transition points. You recall my example of a character's morning routine. As I pointed out before, nobody is interested in the character's waking up, going to the bathroom, taking a shower, dressing, eating breakfast, getting in the car, and going to work. All you have to say is, "The next day Bill drove his Lincoln to work." A good example is in Susan Badavari's novel *Deadly Listing*. The beginning of Chapter 44 starts out with, "Later that evening, Elise sat in a fourth-floor meeting room at the hospital waiting for Matt."

Prologues are at the discretion of the writer. Some writers write prologues to hook the reader. Someone is murdered or dies. If you use a prologue, it should be relatively brief. Whatever kind of prologue you use must engage the reader.

Sometimes you may get bogged down—or downright stuck—in writing the middle of the book. You know how the book has begun and will end, but what do you do in the middle? You deepen the conflict. The more obstacles you create, and the more tension you build, the more the reader

     REVA SPIRO LUXENBERG

will continue burning the midnight oil. That's a cliché. Don't use clichés except in dialogue.

Don't write a book that is didactic. Don't sermonize. Be aware if you are doing it. Leave the sermons to religious leaders. Readers aren't interested in being preached to.

Many times I find authors are redundant. I once read, "He told a false lie." What! A lie, of course, is false.

Finding the right word is a different need. Mark Twain wrote something like, "The difference between the right word (and the wrong word) is the difference between lightning and the lightning bug." Don't get discouraged by how long it takes to write a novel. Just start writing and little by little you'll make progress. You have to go back anyway as the first attempt is a rough draft and you will need to revise. In fact, you will need to revise several times.

CHAPTER 9

Mystery Novels

FROM THE TIME I was a child I have always liked to read mysteries. With great delight I read *Nancy Drew and Her Double Cousin* over and over again. I couldn't get enough of the Nancy Drew books and my closest friend Carol, who was suffering from rheumatic fever, lent me the books that her parents had bought her. As an adult I have read about the master detective Sherlock Holmes created by Sir Arthur Conan Doyle. I've also enjoyed the mysteries of Dame Agatha Christie. It's easy to understand why I began to write mysteries of my own.

A writer of mysteries needs to start with a haunting idea. For instance, as I said before, when I was in Oxford at a writing conference, I surmised that it was a good plan to set a murder in that university town. I didn't know who would be murdered, or who the assassin would be, but Oxford had to be the place. This idea was based on my excitement at being in what I considered was a very exotic location.

I think of a mystery as a novel with one or more dead bodies. Writing one may take days and days of hard work for the author sitting at the computer, all alone—not having fun like going to the movies, on the one hand, and being plagued with self-doubt, on the other. And when the darn thing is finished, most likely the author will get so many rejection letters that she can use them for wallpaper.

However, it's more enjoyable writing mysteries than writing dreary narratives. You get to know your detective, who has all kinds of quirks, and you become intimate with your murderer. You ask why the devil he murders all those people. It's up to you to decide. You're in charge. And if you like to read mysteries—as I do—you won't have that much trouble concocting one.

One good development is that your first mystery may turn into a series. My mysteries are in what are called in the trade "cozy mysteries," because they have a light tone and are fun to read, not because you can curl up in your rocking chair with them—well, maybe that too. Usually the protagonist is an amateur sleuth. I enjoyed reading *Silhouette in Scarlet* by Elizabeth Peters. She skillfully blended comic romantic adventure and an appealing ambience. *Publishers Weekly* praised her this way, "One of Elizabeth Peters' best thrillers yet . . . full of suspense, marvelously evocative, and so funny you will laugh aloud as you read it." If you read more mysteries, gradually you will grasp what makes a good one.

In contrast, I started reading another mystery (which I shall not mention). The author named so many characters that I couldn't keep them straight in my head. Not only did she use a laundry list of characters, she plied her readers with vocabulary that only my husband with his PhD would know. I returned the book to the library. In all fairness to the author, it had an attractive cover.

My mentor Gary Provost, in his book "*100 Ways to Improve Your Writing*," tells about the need to picture the reader. He writes, "Communication occurs in the mind of the reader, and if that reader is not familiar with your terms and your concepts, you might as well write them in Latvian."

There's another reason I like mysteries—it's all about *red herrings*. I do love herring in wine sauce. Just joking. Red herrings are misleading clues, and mysteries are loaded with them. (If you don't like herring, don't write mysteries. Just joking again.)

"Red herring" is a term that originated in the eighteenth century. Dog trainers used pickled herring to distract their tracking hounds, and if the trainee dog ignored the powerful odor and followed the original scent, he was graduated from trainee to graduate dog. I rather think the graduate dog deserved a canine version of a cap and gown on the special day.

The red herring is a trick to keep the reader guessing about what's really going on. In my mystery *The Cereal Killer* I used red herrings to conceal the identity of the murderer. This prolongs the suspense and keeps the reader's attention. It's very effective for sustaining tension. No tension no mystery. Agatha Christie uses enough red herrings to fill a case of jars. She misleads her readers in several books by not revealing gender.

When I started my mystery *Murder at the Second Lily Pond, as* I said before, I didn't know who was going to be murdered and why. All I had was the location. After I left Oxford, I sat down and figured it out. The motivation for the murder has to be plausible. The murderer may kill to right a wrong. Maybe he wants revenge. Maybe he's jealous of an

   REVA SPIRO LUXENBERG

opponent. Maybe he's greedy. Does he want to protect a loved one? Could he be a vigilante?

Before you start, you need to think about the background of both the protagonist and the villain. Give them each good and bad qualities. Then make the crime fit the villain. Would a brawny man use poison? Would a petite woman strangle a tall muscular man?

I like to put my suspects in a single location, as I did in *The Beauty School Murder.* They surrounded the victim in the beauty school when the lights went out. No one saw anything. They were all suspects—even the zany amateur detective.

Agatha Christie adopted the same premise with *Murder on the Orient Express.* It's easier for the writer to have the suspects in the same place as the victim. This can be overused. It should not be done too often.

You need at least three suspects—including the villain. The innocent suspects all have secrets. You make your innocent suspects look guilty by giving them strikes against them such as disappearing, not remembering, having an obvious motive like being blackmailed, eavesdropping, being overeager to answer questions the police put to them, lying, being alcoholics, or manifesting contradictory behavior by claiming to hate the victim but really having complicated opposite feelings. Also your suspects may be in a cutthroat relationship, associate with unsavory people, or have previously committed crimes.

I think a mystery needs more prior planning than a novel. Before you begin, you need to work out a larger amount of facts—like the life of the detective and the villain, the kind of weapon, the number of suspects, the location of the murder or murders, and how the villain is caught.

When I wrote *The Beauty School* Murder, I used the location of a beauty school where I had been a customer. I included my amateur grocery lady sleuth from my other books and wrote another cozy mystery. I had questions I didn't answer—and couldn't—until I got started writing the book. Who was the victim? What were all the characters doing in the beauty school? Who was the killer? What was the motivation? These answers came to me as I kept writing.

If you feature a handgun or a revolver, you should have familiarity with the weapon. Knowing little about guns, my husband wrote a short piece about a man who gets held up in a grocery. He had a right-handed officer pull his gun from the holster on the left side. It doesn't work that way.

In *The Writer's Complete Crime Reference Book*, the author Martin Roth writes, "There are literally thousands of types of firearms, models, and manufacturers, making it impossible to list each make and model." He follows this with a list of twenty handguns and revolvers. Then he lists twenty-three handguns—automatic and semiautomatic. Wouldn't it be easier for you to consider hitting the victim over the head with a rolling pin or killing him with a large kitchen knife? But if you know guns, go with them.

Don't forget to utilize an interesting adversary who causes the protagonist all kinds of problems, like I did in a number of my mysteries when my sleuth herself is suspected of the murder and lands in jail. Lieutenant Detective Salvatore Cagliano is a pain in the neck to Sadie. He was by no means her main challenge, but he did thwart her movement. She

         REVA SPIRO LUXENBERG

provides him with sesame oil to help him with his baldness. That is utter nonsense, but it makes for a lot of laughs.

You owe it to yourself to finish your mystery. You now have a choice. You can put it aside for the rest of your life, or you can go to a writing group to receive constructive critiques. You can try to get it published, or you can self-publish.

Before you do this, re-edit your book. Keep on the lookout for grammatical mistakes, punctuation and spelling errors, overused turns of phrase, stiff dialogue—as well as inconsistencies of names, places, and time and over-long passages of dialogue.

I'm eager to read your mystery.

CHAPTER 10

Memoirs

WRITING ABOUT YOURSELF is easier than writing fiction. One of my stories was published by the Scottsdale Community College and is part of a collection sponsored by the Senior Adult Writing Project there. The book is *Star in the Window: Reminiscences of the World War II Era.* My story "Bensonhurst" appeared in the book with my last name spelled wrong—"*Lurenberg*". I didn't mind, as I was happy to see my work in print. Two writers and I were invited to a special dinner honoring us.

There's a fuzzy line between memoir and autobiography. The latter is a chronological narration of a life's development through the stages of childhood, adolescence, and adulthood. It's written by the main character and is made up of detailed events, places, reactions, and other relevant information. The basis of an autobiography is facts. Gore Vidal clarified the cloudiness thus: "A memoir is how one remembers one's own life, while an autobiography is history, requiring research, dates, and facts double-checked." Who would want to do all this extra work? Not me. Besides I think the memoirs I read in general are more interesting than the autobiographies—with the few exceptions of outstanding individuals.

Memoirs are really less formal and less encompassing than autobiographies. They're more about emotional truth revolving around particular themes of the author's life and her feeling about them. The author writes about herself using the first person. She is not obsessed with factual accuracy.

Sometimes the memories may be painful, as when the writer relives an emotional roller- coaster ride. There are ways writers can ease their own pain and that of the reader. The writer may hurt someone by writing the truth, but that truth can, in fact, be comforting in itself. The rewriting process will provide the emotional distance that's necessary. Writing daily can help bring sharp memories back. The author needs to balance the negative with the positive. A support system can help—friends, family, a teacher, or a fellow writer.

William Zinser, in his book *Writing About Your Life,* says, "No matter how many details you diligently collect about the people and places and events in your past, they won't add up to a memoir." He explains that you need a narrative arrangement. In other words your memoir should read like a novel. The narrative should be so compelling that the readers will stay up all night reading it. It should have tension and momentum. You have to give yourself a plot, a dramatic shape.

You begin by looking at pictures, letters, postcards, diaries, and school yearbooks. You sit at your computer and think of something that's vivid in your memory. You write about it. You describe what happened. You write how you felt at that time. The event should have a beginning, a middle, and an end—just like a short story. Every day you add another memory. It can be one page, two pages, or six pages. You will be amazed at how you'll relive experiences that you thought were irretrievable.

Finally, after you have this collection, you develop your style. It's the unique way you put your words together. Hemingway's style was simple and straight-forward. Style applies to the whole memoir and the way it is written.

You'll also find that you have developed your author's voice. The term 'voice' is the way the author speaks to the world. It comes from deep within the author's soul and heart.

You'll also discover certain themes emerging. You'll begin to see what your memoir is about. Don't use your memoir to whine about your life or to take revenge. Readers don't like that.

If you don't want to have your memoir published, you can take it to Office Max and they'll make a copy for you to give to your children. It's all up to you. But as I have written earlier, don't sell yourself short.

Mary Karr wrote *The Art of Memoir.* She's taught memoir-writing for the last thirty years and she breaks down the key elements of great literary memoir. I don't think it's necessary to aim that high.

With great interest I read Mary Karr's book on this and William Zinsser's *Writing About Your Life.* Both books quote examples of either their own or others' memoirs. I'm quoting a memoir of my own, from my book *Reflections and Recollections.* Notice that it has drama, suspense, and emotion—as well as a beginning, a middle, and an end.

     REVA SPIRO LUXENBERG

ADVANCED ECONOMICS

There was a time in my life I decided I could benefit by matriculatingtoward a Master's Degree in Business. I liked Gregg stenography and I was a capable typist. I wanted to explore another area for me.

A prerequisite course for my business degree was an advanced course in Economics—a breeze I thought. Boy, was I wrong. The professor— I'll call him Mr. Walker—was a soft-spoken middle-aged man. He assigned an Economics book written by Samuelson. Immediately I knew I was in deep trouble. Samuelson was neither Agatha Christie nor Nora Roberts. Although the textbook was written in English, I couldn't make heads or tails of it.

Well, I thought, during his lectures Mr. Walker will explain economics in language I can understand. It didn't happen that way. It was as if the professor was speaking Mandarin. The only thing I understood was when he joked about the Edsel car and what a failure it was. The failure was not only Edsel's but mine. I wondered how the other students in the class were absorbing the information, and I didn't find out until after the first exam.

We had two examinations during the semester and one final examination. On the first exam I received a mark I had never gotten in my entire life—a four percent. I buried my head in my hands and my face reddened like a tomato. I learned that many fellow students had taken other economics courses and passed the exam with high marks.

Subsequently, I studied many hours and days for the next exam and I doubled my mark to an eight percent. Fortunately, kindly Mr. Walker didn't announce the marks to the class. Instead he distributed the tests quietly. I felt like fainting, but didn't collapse, as I wanted to keep my disgrace a secret.

I pondered over what steps I could take so as not to fail this impossible course. For the six years I had been a full-time college student I had never received a failing grade. Finally I came up with the only plan I could devise. I would throw myself on Mr. Walker's possible feelings of compassion and mercy. Another woman might have offered her body, but not me.

At the conclusion of the next to the last class, before the final exam, I approached Mr. Walker while he was still sitting at his desk. "I'm very ashamed of the marks I got on the last two exams. I'm really not a dope, but for the life of me I don't understand our textbook or any of your lectures," I said quietly trying to maintain some degree of poise.

Mr. Walker looked at me with pity in his eyes. "Samuelson is a tough text."

"I never failed a subject. I have a Master's Degree in Social Work. The reason I took this course is that it's required for a Master's in Business. I'd like to have a license to teach typing and stenography. Please tell me if there's a way to prepare for the final?" I held back the tears I felt were starting to form.

Mr. Walker nodded. "I understand your problem. I suggest you study one chapter and memorize it.

 REVA SPIRO LUXENBERG

Whatever questions will be on the final, you write what you have memorized."

I heaved a sigh of relief and followed the professor's suggestion. I passed the course and I will be eternally grateful to this understanding, compassionate man.

P.S. After this, I dropped the idea of a second Master's Degree and I became a school social worker with the Committee on the Handicapped of the New York City Board of Education.

Trisine Rainer, the author of *Your Life as Story*, has a viewpoint counter to mine. She writes, "You will courageously tell the whole truth, because you will love what it does for your writing." I feel, on the contrary, that there are certain parts of your life that require privacy. When you reveal *all* to the world you are taking excessive risks and you leave yourself naked. What I wrote about my failing grades in advanced Economics is amusing—and that was enough. Besides, if I had magnified and multiplied my trials and tribulations, they wouldn't have been the truth.

Trisine Rainer's book is for those hardy souls who want to write a complete literary autobiography of their lives. That's not me, and it may not be true for you as well. But those writers who need to write at length will gain many practical and inspiring messages from her outstanding book.

You don't have to be well-known to describe your life. I have edited a book for a man who had an exciting life, but many lives are exciting each in its own way from different perspectives. Most people go through periods of stress and drama. You don't have to be well-known to describe yours.

CHAPTER 11

Short Stories

SOME AUTHORS FEEL uncomfortable writing short stories and shun doing so. Short-story writing is admittedly tough. I'd rather write a novel. Writing short stories, however, can help a writer grow. It's evident that it takes much less time to write a story than to write a novel of 80,000 words. A short story is under 7,500 words. You will be interested to know that there are outlets for short fiction—like publishing your story as an e-book and entering it in numerous contests. If you write many short stories, you can compile them into a book, as I did in *Reflections and Recollections*.

I tried unsuccessfully to get my mystery story published in *Alfred Hitchcock's Mystery Magazine*. But I did succeed in getting "The Call From Beyond" published by Red Coyote Press in *Medley of Murder: 15 Tales of Mystery and Suspense*. I was overjoyed when my story got an excellent review in the *Scottsdale Republic* newspaper.

The key to a successful short story is its emotional impact. Achieving that is worth the hard work. There's a structure for the short story. It follows an arc and has usually one character who has a concern or a crisis. In some cases you may use a group of characters. The story starts—as in a novel—also with a beginning, follows with a middle, and ends with a bang. You need to get the reader to feel strong emotion. Your setting the stage for maximum effect can be very exacting. You have to pack a lot in a limited time. A quick read doesn't mean less emotional impact. If there's no emotional experience, the story has failed.

If your intent is simply to convey a message, you'd do better to send a telegram by Western Union. A crime story that has an ending with a twist engages the reader's thinking as well as provides entertainment. A literary story about a couple who decide to divorce makes the reader sad.

There are so many different kinds of short stories—a thriller, a mystery, literary, science fiction, crime, or humor. It's your choice.

It's easier to write a short story that sticks to one point of view. Point of view is often written as POV. It can be written in the first person like I wrote in my science fiction story *Inside Out*:

> I spent two weeks with them and found the
> aliens to be quite stubborn. He was getting on
> my nerves. "Driverless cars are air-conditioned,"
> I said." Your moving sidewalks aren't.

Then there's third person, which is more common, as in "Dennis the Menace," in *Reflections and Recollections*.

Mr. Wally Webster sat on his throne in his silk
pajamas in his marble bathroom with its sunken
tub and gold faucets.

Another point of view is the omniscient, which I have never used because I find first and third person more intimate. Writers will use this POV to comment on the characters—often ironically.

In a novel readers will wait patiently for explanations of who the characters are and what action is going to take place. In a short story the writer doesn't have time for that and starts with explanatory material that sets up the story. For example, in "The Vilification of Dr. Mason" in *Reflections and Recollections*, I begin by introducing the character and his location.

The only place where I have a degree of privacy
is in the dank prison library on Riker's Island,
and the only time is just before dinner.

I did insert backstory here to explain how the prisoner came to be a doctor. Usually short stories don't need backstory, but authors will tell you that rules are made to be broken. A word to the wise! Use your own judgment for everything.

If you are inclined to write humorous stories, there are pointers to consider. People like to laugh and you can make them feel good. "Make 'em laugh" is a useful motto.

Comedy is a form of revolt, a breaking of rules. A surprise element produces laughter. The foundation of comedy is *conflict*. The conflict is created by a problem that has to be solved. Two people can strive for the same goal. The question is who will win. The problem can be physical or emotional or both.

There are four levels of conflict: inner conflict, when it's man versus himself; interpersonal conflict, obviously, when it's man versus another person; global conflict takes place when it's man versus the world—meaning his society, his weather, his place, his environment. Cosmic conflict is when it is man versus the cosmic forces like The Lord, Satan, Time, or Fate. We laugh when there's a collision of two different ideas. Resolution is in a surprise punch line, which is often quite powerful. In my short story "Baseball" in *Reflections and Recollections*, I wrote about my going to a baseball game at Ebbets Field between the Brooklyn Dodgers and the New York Yankees. I knew nothing about baseball.

> The odor of the hot dogs and the perspiration from the guy next to me was churning my stomach. Manny bounced in his seat. "There's a ground ball if I ever saw one." *I looked and didn't see a ball on the ground. I was getting bored out of my mind.* "I think this is going to be a perfect game," Manny said, making a fist with his right hand. "I don't think it's perfect," I said. "I believe the players made many mistakes."

I now proceed with some admittedly ignorant remarks about baseball. The sport has conflict and a collision of two opposing takes on a situation. I saw the world of baseball from my unique comic viewpoint of knowing absolutely nothing about it, while I didn't hesitate to make bold, but absurd, observations.

I enjoy writing humor and I try to inject it into my cozy mysteries. You don't have to do that, but I find it's great fun.

There's a need to maintain comic distance, which is the ability to be detached but yet experience the situation vicariously. By having the character have a flaw, you can establish this distance. My flaw in the last example was my ignorance about baseball. Charlie Chaplin used his anti-hero character's ability to thwart authority and that's what made the interaction funny.

You need to add surprise at the end. The reader expects something to happen, but his expectations are reversed. Comedy works on deception. The writer leads the reader into believing one thing and then surprises him with something different.

Humor can have a series of three repetitive events, actions, or dialogue. The first and second times the same thing happens predictably, but the third time is the payoff. It's the unexpected surprise.

Farce is built upon broad improbabilities of plot and characterization more than upon clever wit. Characters may be selfish with exaggerated points of view. They may deal with situations that are chaotic. There may be mistaken identities, ridiculous deception, and shocking revelation. Farce often involves slapstick as in the movie "Home Alone."

I suggest you motivate yourself to read some books about how to write a short story. But do keep in mind that writing short stories is more challenging than writing novels, mysteries, or memoirs.

     REVA SPIRO LUXENBERG

CHAPTER 12

Research

THE RESEARCH I do for my writing unlocks new worlds for me. Even though I'm a senior, inquiry makes me feel young and vibrant. As I said before I utilize the Internet constantly. Even simple topics need research. But I hardly go to my local library because of the easy access to information on the World Wide Web.

You may learn that you can get information by asking folks for help.

Another way to find out things is by observation. One of my mystery-writer acquaintances wanted to know how it felt for a victim to be enclosed in the trunk of a car. Yes, she had her brawny husband stuff her into the car, close the hood, drive a few blocks, and then stop and open the trunk. It's a good thing he was trustworthy. He could easily have done her in and I would never have seen her again.

When I was writing *An Old Lady's Confessions,* I had forgotten the "Senility Prayer." I went online to refresh my memory. "Lord, grant me the senility to forget the people I never liked anyway, the good fortune to run into the ones I do like, and the eyesight to tell the difference."

For my first novel I did a great deal of research about the Holocaust. The more I learned, the more depressed I became. I took my manuscript to the writers' workshop offered by Gary Provost. The first night Gary asked everyone what they were writing. I told him about my suffering protagonist. He said, "She's too passive. You need an active protagonist."

Immediately I abandoned my project and felt like an elephant had been lifted off my chest. I then started my first humorous Sadie Weinstein mystery. Gary loved it and encouraged me. On the last day he put on a doctor's jacket, hung a stethoscope around his neck, and visited everyone in his or her private room with a prescription pad. When he came to my room, he said in his New England accent, "You're the best participant here in your portrayal of character." Then he gave me his "prescription." It read, "Increase description."

 REVA SPIRO LUXENBERG

CHAPTER 13

Writing Groups

I N MY EXPERIENCE there are two polarities among writing groups—helpful and harmful. Some, however, are mixed. I've participated in quite a few where I experienced both sides of the coin. If you put these groups on a balance scale, I believe that the helpful outweigh the harmful.

When I lived in my own home in Sun Lakes, Arizona, I started the Write-Now Critique Group by advertising in the local paper. We met in my living room once every two weeks. At that time I was writing *Grand Army Plaza* about an unlikely pair, an African American boy who is taken care of by a Jewish widow after his mother dies.

Most of the time we were a nucleus of a half-dozen amateur writers. One talented man wrote about adolescent boys in the twenties of the last century. Fraternal female twins argued a lot and wrote in completely different styles. Their arguing was a distraction. That's an example of unhelpful.

A former university professor of English contributed little in the way of his own material, but was helpful with critiques— except that he never praised anyone's work. Another woman with whom I became friends had never written before, but she was a natural writer who submitted good material. I believe she would've been published, but unfortunately she passed away from cancer. She was born in the outback of Australia, and had been a lieutenant in the Australian army when she had been captured by the Japanese. I miss her terribly.

When I moved to Florida, I joined a writers' class. We were given a prompt in class and asked to write for ten minutes. I found this a useful exercise for stimulating my imagination. We were also given homework, a 300 - 500 word piece. The more I wrote the more my writing improved. But there was little critiquing.

A new critique group was formed in a classroom in the clubhouse of my 55+ development. My husband and I attended only once. However, we stuck it out and more writers joined us. I appreciated the critiques I received and in one year I wrote *The Beauty School Murder, An Old Lady's Confessions,* and *The Bumbling Bigamist.* I took on the role of treasurer because we had to have four respective officers— president, vice-president, secretary, and treasurer. I accepted the treasurer's office.

We established rules and procedures of critiquing. Everyone distributed copies of his or her own work. The writer read the piece aloud. Critiques went in clockwise order starting with positive comments before criticism. The president became unavailable and, as it happened, I was elected to take her place.

I handed out the following suggestions for critiquing:

Mention what you love about the writing.
Sections that held your attention.

     REVA SPIRO LUXENBERG

Inconsistencies in Point of View.
Any points of confusion.
More description if needed.
More interaction.
The tension is too prolonged.
Incorrect punctuation.
Needs more action, or less action.
Pacing problem.
Dull narrative.
Weak personalities.
A character may need a goal.
All characters sound the same.
Stilted dialogue.
Implausible story.
Plot not compelling or flowing.
Poor word choices.
Repeated words.
Inconsistency in tense.
Problem with grammar.
Words left out.
Too many words.
Use of clichés .
Spelling mistakes.

Once when I was home sick, my husband led the group. Two new people with axes to grind tore into the work he presented. Immediately the meeting turned into a feeding frenzy, and he came home in an agitated state. This shouldn't have happened. It exemplified "mob psychology" in microcosm. The following time when I was present one of the members of the group said she had unthinkingly joined in with the negative criticism and acknowledged that she felt guilty about it and was sorry. That had certainly been an example of harmful criticism. It is a sad truth that some participants go off on unconscious "power trips." It may even be conscious.

Some critiques cross boundaries into editorializing. Striving for objectivity is necessary. Some people's opinions are uninformed.

I had been vice-president in a number of other groups, but this was the first time I was given the honor of being president. At the following meeting I announced, "The first issue we have to deal with is voting on giving the president a substantial salary. How many vote 'yes'? No one raised his/her hand, but I had "set the tone" with an amusing quip. The day of the meeting was Valentine's Day, which was also my anniversary, and I brought in a box of chocolates. We had reviewed the rules so many times that it wasn't necessary to do so again and also the members were eager to enjoy the treats. We jumped right into the readings.

I conclude with hard-earned advice. If you join a group and it makes you uncomfortable, don't hesitate to look for another more compatible group.

 REVA SPIRO LUXENBERG

CHAPTER 14

Emotional Support

THE FIRST TIME I got real emotional support in a group was at the Writers' Retreat Workshop, I mentioned, run by Gary Provost. I had been to a writing conference in Antioch College where a fellow writer had raved about what an outstanding teacher Gary is. He said with enthusiasm, "If you really want to learn how to write a novel, put yourself in Gary Provost's hands." It wasn't cheap, but I didn't skimp. I spent ten days at a majestic private home in the country in Connecticut, and the whole conference experience was worth every penny. There was something very genuine about Gary and his wife Gail. People at the workshop were drawn to Gary as if he were President of the United States. He knew how to teach writing and he had a wonderful sense of humor. He loved people and they loved him back. People wept when he died. He was lauded in *Writer's Digest* magazine. I'm exceedingly proud to have had Gary as a mentor.

As I have said before, writing is solitary work. The encouragement of others, however, certainly enhances one's self-confidence. I'm lucky to have a husband who praises my work highly. He often says, "This is fabulous." That doesn't mean to say I wouldn't write without his encouragement. I had been a widow for eight years before I married him, and I continued to write. Being productive is a *sine qua non* for me.

If you are lucky enough to have someone in your life who takes an interest in your writing, then don't take him or her for granted. Keep your creative muse delivering.

I'll say for the umpteenth time, in the case of all writing you need to write and re-write many drafts. You must persevere.

My husband met a man who wrote his memoir. It needed a great deal of editing, and he spent many hours improving the work. This man had fascinating and exciting experiences, meeting and befriending famous people in the world of music and entertainment. Not every person leads a life like this, but I believe everyone has something to contribute to the world and many people can write interesting memoirs. Go for it. Finding an editor—just consult one if you need to—will help you progress. If you're single, you may want to find one to marry, as I did. Just kidding, we got married before I knew what a good editor he was.

My point, of course, is that all writers need their work edited. So find an editor you trust, even if you don't want to marry him.

CHAPTER 15

Contests

WINNING WRITING CONTESTS helps a writer step up. There's the prestige that goes with it, the prize, and sometimes publication. Entering contests perks you up and adds adventure to your life. I participated in a nationwide contest when I was eleven. It wasn't connected with writing, but it did have to do with creativity. I drew a map of the United States and sent it into the Stenso Lettering Company. I won third prize, a shiny pair of roller skates. I was also a runner up for a screen play. Both of those wins in my life boosted my self-confidence.

If you go online, there are so many writing contests listed that it's unbelievable. I suggest that it's important to enter contests even if you won't win since you sharpen your skills. Some you have to pay for to enter and some are free. You can submit entries in England and elsewhere. The contests are for short stories, novels, non-fiction, poetry, essays, and a radio play. Some are for fifty words, others for 60,000 words.

Each one has different requirements. I think it's amusing that there are contests that are narrowed down to the locales where you live. Some want only residents who live in the thirteen Southern states. Others ask for writers who live in only in the following states of Washington, Oregon, Idaho, Northern California, Western Montana, British Columbia, and Alaska. Another contest is only for residents of Wisconsin.

There's a contest only for women, others for African Americans, others for "GAYDAR." I had to look this up. It means gay and bisexual men. One contest is only for students. I found one that is unusual in that they plant a tree in Boré, Kenya for every single entry and when the contest is closed and they've received the specifics from their Word Forest Coordinator, they e-mail the GPS coordinates of the individual tree to the respective contributor.

There was a short story contest that requested only 800 words. That appealed to me as I had an apropos theme in mind. I entered the contest online but I never heard back. That didn't discourage me. Don't you be either from writing short stories. The benefit is the shorter time that it takes. If you have many short stories, you can put them in an anthology. Sometimes you may want to expand a story into a novel.

If you write poetry, there are many poetry competitions. One competition for a $1,000 prize stipulated a maximum of only sixty lines.

If you travel a lot, you may enter a travel writing contest seeking either fiction, nonfiction, or an informative essay. They ask for entries between 800 and 5,000 words—which gives you a considerable amount of leeway.

I should mention one famous competition that you'll always see if you subscribe to *Writer's Digest* magazine. It's their Annual Writing Competition, in which the grand prize winner receives $5,000, his or her name on the cover

 REVA SPIRO LUXENBERG

of *Writer's Digest,* and a paid trip to the magazine's annual conference. There are nine categories to choose among. You never know if you'll be a winner. Try it. Like in Vegas—you can't win if you don't play.

CHAPTER 16

Agents

THE *WRITER'S DIGEST* has a "Meet the Agent" page in every issue of the magazine. Information about the agent is given. One woman had supplied details about her favorite author, her blog, fun facts, her dream project, why she does what she does, pitch tips, pet peeves in queries, her range of clients, and contact information. Male agents, of course, are listed as well.

If you go to writers' conventions, you have the opportunity to meet an agent at a writing workshop. I met Donald Maass of the Maass Literary Agency. He deals with mainstream, literary, mystery/suspense, science fiction, and romance. He asked the writers who were present what their favorite movie is. When I answered that it's *A New Leaf* he said I was the first one to give that answer. He offered, "It so happens that it's my favorite, too. I loved its plot and characterization."

I tried to get representation in 2017 by sending out thirty query letters. I was unsuccessful. The nicest rejection letter I received was from Writers House. It said, "I sincerely apologize for the impersonal nature of this reply—we receive hundreds of submissions a month. We wish you all the best of luck in the future."

The Axelrod Agency didn't send me a letter. I received a postcard from them that read, "We are sorry to say that due to commitments to our present clients we cannot offer to read your material." They also wished me ". . . the best of luck in your search for representation."

You can now understand why I go the self-publishing route.

I once had an agent in Hollywood to whom I sent many screenplays. He kept encouraging me, but unfortunately he didn't sell a single one.

It would be wise to seek an agent when you're younger. I was lucky in the casinos when I lived in Arizona, but wasn't lucky finding an agent. The *Writer's Market, Deluxe Edition, 2018* and future editions are an excellent source of listings for book publishers, magazines, contests, and literary agents. They contain advice on writing better queries, making money, and, obviously, getting published.

Another book by Writers Market is *Guide to Literary Agents.* It has instructive material on writing. You can't read enough about writing to guide you down the right path.

I don't like sending out queries as my personal feeling is that it takes time away from my writing books. If I were rich enough to have a secretary, she would do that for me.

I use my old age as an excuse not to send out query letters. But if you're younger than I and want to try to get an agent, I'll give you some tips. When researching an agent, make sure the agent accepts the kind of material you're writing about.

Don't send a query letter to an agent who represents only nonfiction if your manuscript is fiction.

The Sternig & Byrne Literary Agency gives an important tip. They write, "Don't send first drafts, have a professional presentation (including cover letter), and know your field. Read what's been done—good and bad." Now that's a great tip to consider.

When I read that an agency stated, ". . . our current needs are therefore quite limited," I didn't bother to correspond with them.

I did prefer to query by snail mail. I think it's more professional. I always included an "SASE," which is a self-addressed, stamped envelope.

Some agents want a synopsis and the first three chapters. Some want one chapter. Some want a brief bio. Others ask for the entire manuscript, which gets expensive if you keep sending it out.

Your query should be only one page and addressed to a particular agent. Make sure you spell the agent's name correctly. There shouldn't be any spelling mistakes in the letter. That goes for grammatical errors, too.

Start by telling the agent what makes your book unique and interesting. I know of an editor who gives workshops on query letters alone. I think you can write brief query letters yourself. My preference is for double spacing, 12-point type in Calibri font.

I have taught adults in business schools how to write business letters. Follow the form exactly. My husband, however, writes business letters anyway he chooses and he's satisfied with that.

Don't include personal information that's not really related to the book, such as to say how long it took you to write the manuscript. Certainly don't follow the agent around, especially when she goes into the restroom. (Just joking, though I don't doubt people have done that.)

The guides advise you not to phone agents or publishers. I did phone a small publisher once and it turned out she got interested in *The Cereal Killer*. After considering it for a few weeks, however, she rejected it. A reason she gave, believe it or not, was that her husband didn't like the book.

It's appropriate to reveal where you found the agent's name—for example, in a self-help book or on a website. Don't forget to conclude, "Thank you for your attention and time. I look forward to your response." Or, "I appreciate your consideration."

Sign the letter "Sincerely." Underneath your name at the left margin put Enc. and how many enclosures you've included.

I met a young writer who spoke in the library in New Castle, Pennsylvania. She skipped looking for an agent and sent her manuscript directly to a publisher. He accepted it then and now accepts all her books. She writes only fantasy and has created a whole new world. This is an example of rules being broken at one time or another.

It's important to have business cards to distribute. Maybe someone knows someone who has connections. Give out your business cards to people you meet. My card has pictures of books and underneath is the word "Author." I have all my identifying information written in print that's easy to read.

Publishers prepare advertising postcards featuring the book cover on one side and the synopsis on the other side. They also provide business cards and bookmarks. When I pay my household bills, I slip an advertising item into the envelope about my latest book and hope that the clerk will be curious enough to buy the book. If you don't promote yourself, who will?

REVA SPIRO LUXENBERG

CHAPTER 17

Self-Publishing

SINCE I STARTED to write seriously as a senior and I didn't know how long I'd be on this earth, I turned to self-publishing. Yes, it does cost money, but I was determined to create a literary legacy for my heirs. I tried a few publishers and finally settled on one—Xlibris. Since I've begun publishing with them, they consider me a special customer and often offer me a 50% discount for the next book. Often I don't know what I'll be writing about. I take them up on their generous offer. All the packages they provide include copyrighting, the front and back cover design, my bio, and my synopsis, the price of the book, and the service of getting an assigned ISBN number. After the book is published, as I said, they send me postcards, business cards, and bookmarks. They also send laminated posters.

The author may apply for his/her own copyright, which I've done in the past, but it makes life easier by having the publisher secure it. The copyright grants an exclusive legal right to a book for protection against theft—for the lifetime of the author and for a period of seventy years after the author's death. I was once an extra in a movie and I met another extra who complained bitterly that a movie company had stolen his script. Since the script hadn't been copyrighted, he wouldn't have prevailed if he sued.

Some uninformed people think that if they send their completed manuscript to themselves in the mail and don't open the envelope, this covers them. They intend to use the postmark to prove they had written it. That doesn't prove anything.

The ISBN number stands for International Standard Book Number. Its thirteen digits identify the country of origin, the publisher, and the particular edition. Separate numbers are assigned for hard cover, soft cover, and e-books. They're used by booksellers, publishers, librarians, and other interested parties for ordering purposes and cataloguing.

I've met some people who have established their own publishing firm, but I'm not ambitious enough to do this. Maybe "ambitious" isn't the word. I should say "lazy" instead.

The front and back covers of the book are very important, as this is what the reader turns to first in an effort to see if the story interests him. The title and the sub-title (if you have one) belong on the front, including your real name or pseudonym, and usually an attractive picture. One author's memoir that I edited used his nickname, as most of his friends and associates knew him by that name. The back cover is for a synopsis of your book, your biography, and a picture of yourself. It has the publisher's name, the ISBN number, and the price.

When I published *The Call From Beyond And Other Stories* in 2009, I don't remember why I didn't use a picture of the front cover. All my other books have pictures.

          REVA SPIRO LUXENBERG

I took photos of the lily pond in Oxford and used one for *Murder At The Second Lily Pond*. Warning. Don't do what I did. I used a dark blue background for the book, for the front and back cover pages, and the black printing on the back cover is difficult to read.

For *Native American Fun Crafts* I took a picture of a gourd. I dressed it in a woman's Native American costume and that was appropriate for that non-fiction book.

I flew from Arizona, where I was living at the time, to Brooklyn to snap a picture of the central library, the Brooklyn Public Library, which is spotlighted in my *Grand Army Plaza* drama. It's possible I could've acquired a picture in another way, but by going to Brooklyn I was able to see my son and the rest of my family. I used a dark blue background and 14-point font white print.

For *And There Was Light* I took a picture of my silver candlesticks—under a beautiful floral painting on the wall—on a tray on a tablecloth that I had bought in a market in Transylvania. The background color is a dark blue and the white printing is legible.

The murder mystery *The Cereal Killer* needed a special kind of cover. This is a somewhat humorous story about a serial killer who shoots dope pushers and sprinkles cereal on their corpses. You caught the play on words, of course. I paid extra for the publishing company to design the cover and I'm delighted with it. There are different cereals in five bowls that encircle a gun.

Then I engaged Xlibris for my following six books. This publisher has access to thousands of pictures in Thinkstock, the price of which is included in the contract. You select whatever picture is suitable for your book. For my anthology *Reflections And Recollections* I chose a serene path in the woods. The background color is gold and the print is black.

When I published *A Flickering Flame* with Xlibris, I found a picture that depicts the flickering flame of a young man's life. The protagonist died young. The background color is black and the picture is of a hand holding a lit candle.

For the next mystery *The Bumbling Bigamist*— in which the lighthouse in Biloxi, Mississippi, is mentioned—I turned to Thinkstock and found an exact picture of the very lighthouse.

I'm very pleased with the covers that Xlibris has designed.

A blue poison-dart frog is the murder weapon in *The Beauty School Murder.* I chose the picture of the frog from Thinkstock. I believe the cover is perfectly designed. Some of the print is small, and some is large, which is okay with me. I chose a pink background because it contrasts with the image of the blue frog.

My favorite cover is on *An Old Lady's Confessions: Tips For Senior Women.* In Thinkstock I discovered the engaging picture of an old lady with a sly and devilish—but playful and inviting—smile. You can't help but be cheered by this woman.

To give you an idea of how to write a synopsis for the back cover, I'll copy the synopsis of every book that I have published. I don't think you'll mind if I thus give myself plugs. To illustrate that one needs rewrites, I'll confess that I improved the punctuation in several instances. I have found that it's easier to write the entire book than to coax out the just-so synopsis. You'll need to don your thinking cap and spend considerable time getting the book's essence. You need to avoid

  REVA SPIRO LUXENBERG

giving away the ending in the synopsis. You want the reader to be so intrigued that he'll buy your book and read it to the end. Actually one woman told me *The Cereal Killer* robbed her of sleep. That wasn't my intention, but it happened. She really wasn't annoyed, but I said, "I'm sorry," anyway.

THE CALL from BEYOND and OTHER STORIES

This anthology of short stories is a
smorgasbord of humor, mystery,
Biblical lore as interpreted and expanded
by the author, drama,
and science fiction. It is meant to
entertain and bring a smile
to the reader.

MURDER at the SECOND LILY POND

Murder at the Second Lily Pond is a
thoroughly entertaining mystery/
comedy. Sadie Weinstein—cute,
zany, and the most unlikely
sleuth imaginable—gets a call in her grocery in Brooklyn
from her son Jeffrey, a student at Oxford, that he has been
arrested for the murder of his archaeology
don. After she *shlepps* to
Oxford, along with her husband
Nathan, to free her son, she gets
involved in a flirtation with Sir Donald Ward, Assistant

Commissioner of Scotland Yard, is
accused of murder, adopts a cat
she names Inspector Ebony, and sets a fire, all in the
course of the investigative process.

NATIVE AMERICAN FUN CRAFTS

If you enjoy making unusual crafts, this
book is for you. The theme
is Native American and the materials
are different—like a brown egg
for a face and a prune container for the gourd to
stand on. The author tells you where to
buy the supplies. The directions are
easy to understand and the resulting
crafts make great gifts.

GRAND ARMY PLAZA

When creative and intelligent Jamal Holden's mother dies,
the eleven year-old becomes a guest in Chaya
Bloom's apartment. This leads to a cultural collision
that rocks the apartment house in the mixed-
race neighborhood of Crown Heights in Brooklyn.
Jamal has to exchange his love of sweet potato pie
for gefilte fish, while Chaya has to defend her values
to her intolerant married daughter and hostile neighbors,
even as she struggles with the question of whether
she should adopt a child of another color and religion.

 REVA SPIRO LUXENBERG

AND THERE WAS LIGHT

Malka, at 18—pretty and tortured by
low self-esteem—makes the
biggest mistake of her life by allowing
her family to dictate when
and whom she should marry. Struggling
with the practices of her
Orthodox Jewish faith, she alienates her family. An unlikely
mentor, Ariana, a high-paid model who
lives in Greenwich Village,
steps in to help her with her metamorphosis from the plain
caterpillar to a rebellious butterfly.
Malka becomes Marci as she
copes with her stern father, an unknown secular world, the
possibility of having AIDS, her failed marriage,
and her subsequent courtship.

THE CEREAL KILLER

Sadie Weinstein, wife and joint owner
with her husband Nathan of
Weinstein's Grocery, is a wacky amateur detective
modeling herself after Agatha Christie's Hercule Poirot and
Miss Marple. She enlists the help of her
"Cereal Killer Squad" in her
quest to aid the police capture the
infamous "Cereal Killer," who
murders dope pushers and sprinkles cereal on their bodies.
Nathan has his doubts about the squad—with its

two prostitutes, a guidance counselor, an aunt of a victim,
and an Indian psychic—but zany Sadie doesn't heed
his warning. Her persistent sleuthing
fails to yield a single clue until
she comes face to face with the perpetrator,
who finally has to face the
consequences of the murders.

REFLECTIONS and RECOLLECTIONS

Reflections and Recollections is a delightful
collection of imaginative
stories. It contains memoirs and poems—
some of which are hilarious.
Once you start reading the book you
won't want to put it down. The
section on memoirs is unusual, to say
the least, as the author describes
her brief relationship with boxer Tommy
"Hurricane" Jackson and her
close call in almost burning down the
Empire State Building. This is
a book you might enjoy reading over many sittings.

A FLICKERING FLAME

A Flickering Flame is a compelling tale
about Jeffrey Shulman, a

       REVA SPIRO LUXENBERG

brilliant pathological liar, an emotionally
scarred man with a rare
condition named by psychiatrists as
pseudologia fantastica. It is
an engrossing chronicle of his life—
from his infancy when he was
abused, to when he becomes a convincing
imposter, to his wife's
attempts to murder him with a .357 magnum,
and to his subsequent struggle to survive
and get custody of his children.

THE BUMBLING BIGAMIST

Sadie Weinstein runs a mom-and-pop
grocery in Brooklyn in 1969
with her husband Nathan. A quirky
amateur detective, she persists
in solving a murder that takes place
when she is present at a home
in Staten Island. The murdered victim
is a bigamist who had two
wives, and possibly more, in different
far-removed locations. Sadie
tracks down suspects from Rutgers
University in New Brunswick,
New Jersey, and as far away as Biloxi,
Mississippi. Sadie becomes a suspect
herself and must solve the mystery
to clear her name. Nathan

warns her constantly not to "stick her neck out," but she is
undeterred. Her charming pickle-
eating customer and psychic
Rhajmah has revealing visions. The
excitement mounts in Biloxi
during the savage onslaught of
Hurricane Camille. The story
involves anguish, but Sadie's antics
and repartees lighten tension.
This is a gripping Sadie Weinstein
mystery, Luxenberg's fourth.

THE BEAUTY SCHOOL MURDER

There are four suspects in the beauty
school murder in Florida. Sadie
Weinstein, the quirky amateur sleuth
who owns a mom-and-pop
grocery in Brooklyn with her husband
Nathan, is the primary
suspect. Sadie prevails upon her reluctant
spouse to help her entrap
the murderer. She also contacts Rhajmah, her psychic
and pickle-eating customer and friend, to
help her unravel the mystery and keep
her out of jail. She needs all
her skill, energy, ingenuity, eccentricity,
and Poirot-like grey cells to
succeed. *The Beauty School Murder* is an expansion of
an earlier version of the cozy mystery, *Curl Up and Die.*

          REVA SPIRO LUXENBERG

AN OLD LADY'S CONFESSIONS: TIPS for SENIOR WOMEN

The author is a senior citizen who has
the desire to share some of
her experiences and practical down-to-
earth knowledge with other
mature women. The book covers
relationships with children and
husbands and advice about mind and
body that includes senior
moments, food, clothes, skin, and
care of nails and hair. The
author talks about weight, interests,
finance, cleaning, medical
and age discrimination, and housing—
and concludes with hints for
making travel easier and more pleasurable.
Mrs. Luxenberg trusts
that older women will benefit from her suggestions.

If you happen to have relatives who recommend you to
an agent who then gets you to a publisher, you're a lucky
so-and-so. If your query opens the door, then you don't need
to go my self-publishing route. If you do need to be self-
published, there's no shame in that. Self-publishing is here
to stay!

CHAPTER 18

Success

THERE ARE MANY definitions of success. At my time of life success is getting up in the morning and thanking God for being alive. As far as writing goes, success doesn't mean being like Nora Roberts or Stephen King. For me it's getting my books published and having some readers enjoy them. I encourage people who want to write. Just keep writing and you'll improve. Self-publishing is a simple way to have your book published. Holding your book in your hand builds your self-confidence. Self-publishing one book, furthermore, increases your motivation to publish additional ones. Your friends and family salute you for your effort. Of course, it takes a lot of that.

Five individuals I admire define success in their own unique ways.

Albert Schweitzer says, "Success is not the key to happiness. Happiness is the key to success. If you love what you are doing, you will be successful." He wasn't talking about material gain, but about how much love you put into your labor.

Mother Teresa said the same thing in different words. "It's not about how much you do, but how much love you put into what you do that counts." I say if you write a book and you put love into it, you're successful.

Dale Carnegie has another twist. "People rarely succeed unless they have fun in what they are doing." When I first started out, writing was more hard work for me than fun, but in time I realized that writing was indeed quite enjoyable. When I'm tired, my writing drags, so I stop until I feel more energetic.

Lee Iacocca, the American car executive known for spearheading the development of Ford Mustang and Pinto cars stated, "You've got to say, I think that if I keep working at this and want it badly enough, I can have it. It's called perseverance." How true. Without perseverance I never would've finished all the books I've written. If you truly want to be a writer, you have to write and not worry about it. Just do it!

The gal I admire for a really successful life is Oprah Winfrey. I don't have to tell you who she is and what she has accomplished. She says, "The essential question is not, "How busy are you?" but "What are you busy at?" I've seen young men and young women and kids, too, talk a very great deal on I-phones. They may want to write, but they're too preoccupied with their conversations. They'd be better off in writing groups writing and talking to each other about what they have written.

The media and society have placed the definition of success in our minds as having to do with wealth, power, and material possessions. We watch the ads on TV and wonder when we'll have the rich home, the expensive exercise equipment, and the dream vacation. Isn't success about living our dream in writing, enjoying the present moment, and living up to our potential?

As I said before, I'm an admirer of Agatha Christie. I read in *Agatha Christie's Secret Notebooks* by John Curran, "Christie's prose, while by no means distinguished, flows easily; the characters are believable and differentiated; and much of the book (*They Came to Baghdad*) is told in dialogue." For sure, Christie was a writing success. It makes no difference if one critic may have opined that her prose is not elegant. Millions of discriminating readers have found her books to be well-written indeed.

Don't put much thought into becoming a successful writer. Just write for the joy of it. Readers may well appreciate greatly what you have written.

In the March/April 2018 edition of Writer's Digest magazine, Suanne Laqueur says in answer to the question about the best writing and/or publishing advice she had received, "My editor told me, 'Just tell the story. Don't be clever, and get out of your own way. Say what happens. Say what you mean.'"

Be willing to educate yourself. You may need to improve your vocabulary, your grammar, and your punctuation. Strive for honesty in what you write. Be authentic. There's a growing demand for books about diversity in culture, race, and gender. You don't have to be a scholar like my husband to write. I never considered myself a scholar. I didn't graduate from Harvard like he did. My books in turn reach a wider range of people than his.

Chicken Soup for the Soul is an example of positive thinking and perseverance. Co-authors Jack Canfield and Mark Victor

Hansen had focus and determination when they first started out. They fulfilled their dream with tremendous perseverance to land a publisher finally after the 143 times they had been rejected. They were successful the 144th time. If they had given up after twenty times or seventy-five times, readers wouldn't have their books to enjoy. What interests me is that they didn't actually write these books, they just sponsored them. There are now over 250 inspiring Chicken Soup books. At a writing conference I was stirred from my head down to the tips of my toes listening to Jack Canfield's motivational speech there.

Start by learning the craft of writing and investing necessary work time and effort to apply what you've learned, while keeping your attitude positive. Nothing ventured—nothing gained.

Whether your book is commercially published or self-published, you can ask if you may give a presentation on it at your local library.

When I lived both in New Castle, Pennsylvania and in Scottsdale, Arizona, I asked the local newspaper editor if they would do a feature on me and the book I had just published. It was serendipitous when a team took a picture of me in my home, interviewed me, and wrote an article on the book and on me.

I close by contrasting a wildly acclaimed author with an unsung one. I met Harlan Coben, a tall imposing figure of a man, when he spoke at the Poison Pen bookstore in Phoenix, Arizona. At that time he was writing about a basketball player turned sports agent Myron Bolitar, who was investigating murders. Since the only sport I'm interested in is golf, I had only read a couple of his sports-agent thrillers. Harlan Coben kept writing until he won an Edgar Award, a Shamus Award, and an Anthony award. He is the first writer to have received all three. Seventy million of his books are in print worldwide. The last book I read by him *Fool Me Once* is another #1 *New York Times* bestseller. There is no doubt that Harlan Coben is a success as far as recognition goes.

However, there's another author I admire who wrote only one book, *Overbooked in Arizona* by Samuel Hirsh Gottlieb, a novella of ninety-five pages. I consider it the most amusing book I have ever read. I laughed all the way through this wildly funny tale of a book collector who gets executed for murder. My judging Samuel Hirsh Gottlieb a success is subjective, but I bet that, if you read this book, you will agree with me.

You too can achieve writing success. I send you my very best wishes, and I look forward to seeing your work in print. I wish you the material success of Coben, and if you don't achieve that (how many people do?) the fulfillment of both Coben and Gottlieb, and countless less-acclaimed writers have experienced. Good luck!

   REVA SPIRO LUXENBERG

www.ingramcontent.com/pod-product-compliance
Lightning Source LLC
Chambersburg PA
CBHW031409250726
48656CB00002B/609